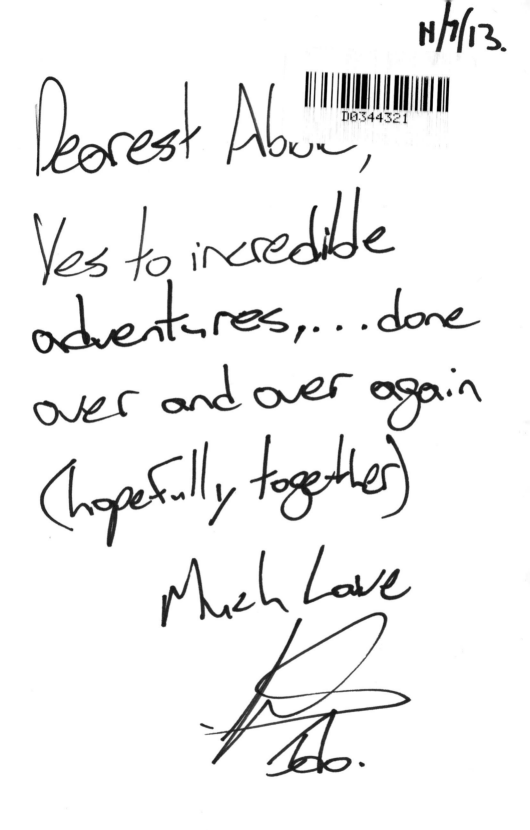

Get Big Fast and Do More Good

GET BIG
FAST
— and —
DO MORE
GOOD

Start Your Business, Make It Huge,
and Change the World

Ido Leffler
and Lance Kalish

New Harvest
Houghton Mifflin Harcourt
BOSTON   NEW YORK
2013

www.hmhbooks.com

Library of Congress Cataloging-in-Publication Data
Kalish, Lance.
Get big fast and do more good / Lance Kalish and Ido Leffler.
pages cm
Includes index.
ISBN 978-0-544-11448-7
1. Entrepreneurship. 2. New business enterprises. 3. Social responsibility of business.
I. Leffler, Ido. II. Title.
HB615.K353 2013
658.1'1 — dc23
2013010481

Book design by Brian Moore

Printed in the United States of America
DOC 10 9 8 7 6 5 4 3 2 1

To our wives, Ronit and Loren, and kids, Zoe and Emi (Ido's) and Ethan and Claudia (Lance's), we dedicate this book in your honor.

Contents

Foreword

Dream more than others think practical. Expect more than others
think possible. Care more than others think wise.

— HOWARD SCHULTZ, FOUNDER OF STARBUCKS

H ow do you build a multimillion dollar global business?
Well, you might start by visiting Israel and negotiating the
rights to an unknown brand (Yes To Carrots) . . . found in only sixteen stores. Then, you might use cold-calling artistry and Jedi mind
tricks to get the product carried by Walgreens in its seven thousand-
plus stores. Next, you might get your product into more than twenty-
five thousand stores internationally and smile when you see Rosario
Dawson using your goods publicly. Now, as the happy ending (of
sorts), every six seconds in the United States someone buys a Yes To
product!

But that's leaving out the details, isn't it? I hate business books that
do that.

And that's why this book was written — to tell the detailed story of
Yes To's improbable rise, including the stupid mistakes, near-fatal ca-

tastrophes, existential crises, and fancy sales footwork. In short, the real story of entrepreneurship.

I've known Ido Leffler, Yes To's cofounder, for ages. I met him at a Summit Series event in Miami. His trademark hug was the first thing that caught my attention: inexplicably slow-motion and super gentle, as if he were cradling a baby panda. Of course, there's his subtle Australian accent and persuasive (and deliberately less subtle) Israeli chutzpah. Who the hell was this guy? I've come to love him, but perhaps more important to you, I've come to love his methods. He deconstructs problems like Sherlock Holmes with a twist of Richard Branson.

As I learned from this very book, his partner, Lance Kalish, is even more methodical. In many respects, he is to Ido what Steve Wozniak was to Steve Jobs. That's part of the reason their partnership works. To paraphrase one of Yes To's investors: "He [Lance] is the numbers guy, and he [Ido] is the pictures guy."

In the following pages, you will learn how both of them went from selling out of a suitcase to building the second-largest and fastest-growing natural beauty brand in the United States, with almost one hundred unique products (or SKUs, pronounced "skews"). More specifically, you will get the inside baseball on how they:

- negotiated the rights to Yes To Carrots and what you should consider when looking for similar hidden gems,
- pitched and won their largest marquee customers, including Walgreens and Target,
- contacted impossible-to-reach CEOs and decision makers to make magic happen,
- courted and selected investors, both in the beginning and when they became massive,

- decided to be cofounders (hint: think "allies" over "friends"),
- rebounded from failed products and various disasters, and
- hired a CEO once they decided to leave day-to-day management.

I was tempted to write that this book is a beautiful example of the American dream. But that's not exactly true.

It's the Australian dream.

It's the British dream.

It's the Indian dream.

It's the [fill in the blank] dream.

Ido and Lance's story is the dream of doers everywhere—the dream of making something happen, of creating something meaningful from nothing.

Have you ever had a job and thought, "I could do a better job than this guy," while watching your boss? Have you ever thought of an invention for solving a common problem and asked, "Why hasn't someone *done* this yet?" If so, you've found the right book.

In closing, I could say, "May the wind always be at your back," but that's not how this game works.

Instead, I'll recommend that you gird up your loins (figuratively), grab a cup of coffee, and prepare for an adventure. This is just the beginning.

Enjoy the ride,

TIM FERRISS
BUENOS AIRES
MAY 2013

Introduction

HI! WELCOME TO OUR BOOK, *Get Big Fast and Do More Good.* We're going to explain how two schmucks built a global brand out of nothing in less than five years and, of course, how you can do it, too.

But before we do that, we need to give you a little background on who we are and how we get things done. Lots of people know Ido; he's the public face of our company, the one who wears orange no matter what and makes CNBC anchors laugh in spite of themselves. Lance is the wizard behind the curtain, happy to pull the levers when needed and just as glad to be out of the spotlight. Together, we form a strong and well-balanced partnership.

Admittedly, we've had a few disagreements during the writing of this book. One of the first was over the title. Ido wanted to call it *Big, Fast, and Good,* but Lance thought that sounded like a porn movie. Ido told Lance he didn't have a sense of humor, and Lance told Ido he wasn't literate enough to read a book, let alone name one. Eventually, we settled on something that was better than either of us could have come up with on our own.

Get Big Fast and Do More Good is our philosophy toward business and life. It has always been our goal to create a brand, grow it quickly, and make the world a better place in the process. Why? Well, it has to be *big* because a product that nobody's heard of isn't going to change the world. It has to be *good* because only companies that try to make the world a better place deserve to succeed. And it has to be *fast* because we like to move fast, and because we still have a ton of things we want to do with our lives. We love Yes To, but Ido wants to retire to Tel Aviv while he still looks good in his swim trunks, while Lance is planning on managing Manchester United at some point in the near future.

When we started, we were looking for an accelerated way to succeed in life. One option was to do what our parents wanted us to do: Pick a profession (i.e., medicine or law), stay focused, study hard, work diligently, and make as much money as possible for forty years, then retire and actually start to enjoy our lives. This approach is great. The world needs doctors and lawyers. *We* need doctors and lawyers all the time, in fact, whether it's to mend a soccer injury (Lance) or get out of a speeding ticket (Ido). Cheers to you, MDs and JDs. We're glad you all had the focus and single-mindedness for your respective paths. We're also so, so glad we *didn't*.

The other way to succeed — what we like to call the Yes To way — is less straightforward than the professional path. There are no classes, exams, or cram sessions. You don't get a grade and you don't graduate with a degree. The path is filled with questionable decisions, Hail Mary moves, and bank accounts that are sometimes down to one rent check, half a phone bill, and a kebab. It can be pretty scary, frankly.

So why do it? As risky as the entrepreneur's life can occasionally seem, it can also be amazingly rewarding and incredibly good fun. Over the last ten years, we've made every possible mistake, and also taken a few gambles that have paid off big. We've almost lost our business a couple of times, and we've had moments where the entire future of Yes To has hung on a last-minute meeting with a stranger on the other side of the world.

Scary, yes. But also breathtaking. We're both gamblers by nature, as are most successful entrepreneurs. We have faith in ourselves and in our ideas, and because of this we can tolerate the risks that sometimes lead to big rewards.

Get Big Fast and Do More Good is our guide to becoming a better entrepreneur. Our goal is to show you that you don't have to be some kind of infallible superhero to succeed in business. Being the smartest person in the room is less important than getting the basics right and being truly passionate about your business.

We were each lucky to have an optimal blend of supportive parents, happy childhoods, and unexpected and very difficult family setbacks. Our families gave us confidence and optimism; our struggles made us grow up fast and full of determination. We've both spent significant parts of our lives in third-world countries and start-up economies; this has given us a real appreciation for the sheer *nachas** that comes from making big and improbable things happen.

For the first five years of our business, we were nomads, living all over the world, from London to Sydney to the beautiful beaches of Tel Aviv. Ido spent so much time on Qantas, United, and Virgin Atlantic 747s, they might as well have had a doormat on the plane saying, "Welcome Home." We had a company policy of buying only round-the-world plane tickets; they worked out cheaper and made it possible for us to use our patented "one-day window" technique to schedule high-level meetings (see chapter two). And in all the rushing back and forth, we made many, many mistakes, from deciding to become guinea pigs for an herbal version of Viagra (almost ending Ido's love life permanently) to misreading our first big order (by a factor of ten).

---

* Yiddish for "joy"

Before we get started, here are a few key facts about us:

- Ido is the good-looking one. Lance disputes this.
- Lance is much, much better at soccer than Ido. Ido disputes this.
- Ido wears orange every day. Lance wears "Dad jeans" every day.
- Lance is numbers. Ido is pictures.
- Ido spent years annoyed that Lance wanted to leave the office at 6 p.m. to "get home to his kids." Now, he has kids himself and he's out the door at 5 p.m.

We are serious about our business and our families, and light-hearted about everything else. So long as we are enjoying our time on earth and our kids have a roof over their heads, nothing else really matters. As you read *Get Big Fast and Do More Good*, we'll keep reminding you how important it is to enjoy life. All the success in the

world means nothing if your family is unhappy, or if your spouse feels neglected. Success is easy come, easy go. So is money. But you have only one family. And when things fall apart, you will need that strong, supportive, and united group to help you rebuild.

We hope you enjoy the stories in this book, and finish it inspired to apply our lessons to your own business and life. After all, if two guys like us can get this far, this fast, what the hell is stopping you?

1

And in the Beginning . . .

Scene: 9:01a.m., Yes To offices, San Francisco, late 2012

WHEN WE FIRST DECIDED TO sit down and write our book, we got the same great advice on storytelling from various authors and agents and editors: "Start at the beginning and end at the end!" So naturally we are going to ignore that advice and do the opposite. In fact, we are going to spoil the whole thing right now and tell you what happens on the last page of the Yes To story:

Everything works out really well!

As you'll see, we've gone through some pretty crazy stuff over the last six years, but the payoff has been worth it. We have a company that has survived the recession and is now thriving in the recovery. Lance tells anyone who will listen how Organic Monitor, a leading international market research firm, specifically recognized Yes To for changing the U.S. beauty consumer's perception of natural products from "alternative" to "popular." We both have the personal lives we'd always dreamed of: happy kids, nice homes, and wives who willingly and frequently talk to us!

If you visit us in our offices in San Francisco you'll find a small but dedicated group of people who operate more like an extended family than a bunch of employees. There are around thirty of us, which is nothing when you consider the amount of business we do. A more traditional company would have five times the staff. As a company, we are light and nimble on our feet; as a result, we can react very quickly to both opportunities and problems, and we want to keep things that way.

Why base ourselves in San Francisco? From the beginning, we were as much a high-tech start-up as a beauty brand. Our goal was always to apply our very modern sensibilities to a somewhat old-fashioned industry and develop a new business model that worked.

Eight years ago, Yes To was a novelty product manufactured in Israel and sold in about ten outlets there. We saw something special in this quirky little line, partnered, and remade it to fit our own vision of what a modern beauty brand should be. Now we are carried in 25,000 stores across twenty-five countries including retailers such as Target, Walgreens, and Walmart. We've gone from six products to almost eighty, and from being an unknown newcomer to number two in the natural-beauty category. Three years after our U.S. launch, we started to overtake our well-established and highly aggressive competitors. Our sprint to the top shook up the heritage natural brands and changed the way natural products come to market. We're proud to say we made our whole industry start to think differently about the category.*

Along the way, we've learned one hugely important lesson: We are positive people, and our company has to reflect that. We can compro-

---

* Yes To is the number two natural brand by dollar sales in FDMx, growing 21 percent year over year. (Source: Nielsen FDMx, P52 weeks ending 10/27/12)

mise on the amount of sleep we get or the speed of a product roll-out, but we can't compromise on being a company that does, and is, "good." What does "good" mean to us? It is, very simply, operating a business in an ethical, moral way with equal regard to our consumers, our partners, the environment, and the well-being of everyone involved in the production of our products. We each have children, and we want those kids to grow up in a healthy, positive world. That means our company has to operate by certain standards, even when it costs more and causes more difficulty than other, less positive approaches. Too many businesses seem to think that they have to do negative — be it avoid environmental regulations or pay their employees the lowest wages possible — things to make their investors or stockholders happy; we think this attitude is nonsense. Investors need clean air and water as badly as the rest of us. Why not incorporate "good" into your business model right at the start, when your business is just a dream? Why not build the idea of giving back into your brand's DNA, even when your brand is just you, a cup of coffee, and a laptop?

We hope this book inspires you to look for opportunities in unexpected places and to realize that you don't have to go to the best business school (or indeed any business school at all) to learn the entrepreneurial skills that will allow you to succeed. Success isn't that hard; it's the screw-ups and "oh, crap!" moments that will really test you. We've had plenty of those, and we're still here. You will be too.

And now, back to the beginning!

A Tale of Two Schmucks

We are many things: business owners, investors, parents, husbands, sons, and friends. But at the very core, in our hearts, we are and always have been entrepreneurs. Entrepreneurship isn't for everyone, but if you have the nerve, we think being an entrepreneur is in many ways a safer and better way to approach your career than conventional employment.

So, how do you go about becoming an entrepreneur? We think the whole idea of nature versus nurture is a bit of a cliché. Successful entrepreneurs regularly come from unexpected backgrounds and experiences, and they just as frequently *don't* materialize in places you would expect to find them. For every Mark Zuckerberg, there are a thousand Harvard grads working in conventional careers, often with great professional success but no obvious entrepreneurial ambitions. Likewise, there are people like Bernie Ecclestone, who was born into an impoverished family in England, left school to become a mechanic, and managed to parlay that into a position ruling the Formula One racing franchise (where he made billions).

Entrepreneurs: You never know where you'll find 'em.

What does it take to create that entrepreneur mentality? Let's suppose you weren't raised in as optimal a petri dish as we were. Perhaps your parents weren't businesspeople, or they were never particularly supportive of your dreams and ambitions. In this chapter we are going to share some of our most pivotal moments. Now, we're not telling you these stories merely because we are wildly charismatic and interesting people and you'd be nuts *not* to want to know more about us. We're sharing them because each of these moments contributed in some way to making us better entrepreneurs.

One thing you'll hear from us a lot is the value of having good accents and, frankly, we have *fantastic* accents. Ido's is a confidently authoritative Israeli that accelerates into an excitable and earnest Silicon Valley-ese when he's talking about Yes To and takes on the hint of an Australian twang when he's finally back home with his family. Lance's chilled-out Australian accent morphs into a considerably more assertive Jo'burg inflection when he's talking politics. A great accent will impress girls, get you out of speeding tickets (and even tricky situations at customs), and generally make people pause for a second before saying no. If you are smart and fast, you can take that pause and turn it into an opportunity.

Our enthusiasm for funny accents is just a small part of our bigger life philosophy: Don't be afraid to be the odd kid. Both of us went through being the odd, out-of-place, new kid, and somehow those experiences gave us both a huge amount of confidence in ourselves and our abilities.

Ido left Israel for Australia when he was four, the age when you are taking your first few steps of independence from your parents, making your own friends, and generally breaking into the world as a child. Lance left South Africa for Australia when he was nineteen, the age when you are leaving your family home and taking your first steps outside of it as an adult. Lance wanted to seem cool and independent, but in reality he was just a kid with a funny accent and some truly terrible apartheid-sanction-era clothes.

Profound changes like these force you to do more; if we'd emigrated when we were one or two years of age, we'd just have blended in. Coming to a country later in life means you have to build your platform as a human being. You have to figure out who you are, how you present yourself to your potential friends, and what your story is. In other words, you have to build your own brand and market the hell out of it if you want some mates in the pub or on the playground. After all, as the odd kid you're going to stand out no matter what. It's up to you to make the most of it.

Australia welcomed a huge influx of South African immigrants in the eighties and nineties. Newcomers had to decide pretty quickly if they were going to adapt to their new reality — life in Australia — or cling to memories of the old life they'd left behind.

We embraced change. We both have friends who arrived at the

same time we did but never really assimilated into Australian culture. Instead, they stuck with the behavior and fashions of their old life. It's important to stay connected to your old community, but it's also important to become part of the local scene. Being able to be part of more than one world at a time is an incredible skill, useful in both your personal and professional life. And these kinds of big changes give you a fantastic opportunity to change your trajectory.

Even if you've lived in the same house on the same street since the day you were born, you can still make a conscious decision to create an identity that sets you apart and attracts you the positive attention you'll need to succeed. If you can, beg, borrow, or save two grand, get on a plane to a randomly chosen Asian country, and live off twenty bucks a day for a few months. Try being a "different" person and see what you learn from the experience.

Ido: I was born in Israel in 1977. Israel is a small pressure cooker of a country. I love Tel Aviv; it's full of noise and color and the kind of intensified energy and emotion that comes with knowing things can get dangerous very quickly. The city has a palpable creative energy. People don't waste time, and there is a real pressure to do something big with your life. The flip side is that you're also dealing with the constant unknown of where and when something unexpected will happen.

My dad was a robotics engineer. When I was four years old, he moved our family to Australia for a two-year contract. Of course, once you get to Sydney, it's hard to leave; we loved the great weather, the positive people, and the exquisite surroundings. After the constant stress of living in Israel, it was incredible to live in a country where the only things you had to look out for were spiders, snakes, sharks, and jellyfish.

Before the first year was up it was clear we were never going home.

Some people are inspired to take risks because their parents never did. Some carry on a family tradition of taking chances on long odds.

For me it was a mix: My parents made conventional career choices in Israel, but once they got to Australia they were inspired to dream bigger. My dad quickly realized there was a cap on how much money he'd ever make as an engineer. A friend of his was making a fortune excavating, so my dad quit engineering, bought a truck and a Bobcat, and started driving them himself.

Eventually, my dad became even more ambitious. He found an ugly little house on a great piece of land, knocked it down, and built a palatial new home in its place. (Like everyone else in the world, my dad had contracted the real estate bug.) He and his partner decided to make one big investment and build a house that they would sell for seven million dollars.

You'll notice that this story is being told in the past tense. Right when my dad put all his capital into the house, Australia went through one of the worst housing recessions in its history. The value of homes halved, interest rates went from single digits to high double digits, and my parents lost everything.

Here's the point of my story: I was twelve when we went from wealthy to broke. The day they found out, my parents drove to school to pick me and my brother up, and we sat in our Mitsubishi in the school parking lot while they told us everything that had happened and the whole truth about what we had lost. I don't think it occurred to them to try and hide any of it.

Good or bad, my family was in this thing together.

Now that I'm a parent myself, I can appreciate how brave and wise they were to be so honest with us. Knowing the truth about our family's situation made us grow up fast, but it also made us feel incredibly bonded to our parents and determined to pull our weight and help get our family through this disaster. I do the same thing now: Good or bad, my family will always know the truth about what's happening. Ditto with my employees.

Realizing You Want to Run the Game, Not Play It

Lance: I grew up in apartheid-era South Africa. My family was very happy there for years. However, by the early nineties it was incredibly dangerous. Unfortunately, as young kids we were more or less oblivious to the miserable conditions that our black neighbors endured. My family had a big house in a safe suburb, and like most other families we had nannies and gardeners and maids. My nanny was a funny, no-nonsense woman named Sarah. Her way of taking care of me when I was young was to strap me to her back with blankets in the traditional African style and get on with her life.

The highlight of the nannies' workday was playing a game called fafi. Fafi was basically a numbers racket, rumored to be run by the Triads (the local Chinese mafia). Every Monday, Sarah would sneak me out of the house and we would walk to the corner. She and I and the other nannies would wait there for a rusted, beat-up van to arrive. The door would slide open, and a pair of hands would emerge from the gloom to take the nannies' bets and hand out small amounts of cash to last week's winners. A twenty-five-cent bet paid out twenty-five rand, roughly a week's wages. It was hugely popular because you needed to bet only a small amount of money and your chances of winning were relatively good.

When I was ten, I decided this easy money was a great thing and that I wanted in on it. The next time we went, I gave Sarah all of my pocket money and she placed a bet for me. The guys running the game were smart; the first time I played, I won. Right away I was hooked. Clearly, I had some special, intuitive skill that allowed me to beat these gangsters at their own game.

I decided I needed to play a bigger game for a bigger return, and this required more cash than my meager pocket money. I knew of only one source of ready cash in the house, so when my mum wasn't looking I rifled through her change jar for a handful of coins. My mum was either not observant enough to notice or too kind to mention the small amounts of money I pilfered to up my stakes. Either way, my parents never knew that I was a committed gambler, and at the age of ten occasionally indebted to China's most deadly gangsters. I may have looked like just another schoolboy, but I was convinced I could beat their system and figure out a way to win the numbers racket.

Sorry, Mum.

I would love to be able to tell the inspiring story of a young boy and his South African nanny beating the Triads, but no such luck. My first win was also my last, and I quickly realized that I didn't like being on the losing end of the deal.

After daydreaming about what *my* numbers game might look like, I decided that running a rival racket up against some pretty scary characters was not a great life choice for a ten-year-old to make.

As they say, "The house always wins." It's the same thing in business. Do you want to be the person who owns the idea or the product and sets the terms by which it is sold or the person who's hired to sell, market, or distribute that idea or product? There's nothing wrong with either choice, but it's important to know where you will work best and find the most success. My short-lived career as a high-stakes preteen gambler taught me that I wanted to be the guy running the game, not playing it, and I live by that lesson to this day.

Ido: I have to speak up here. Regardless of what Lance says, I've been to Vegas with him on a number of occasions. Inevitably, we have a few drinks, and then he drags me to the poker table in the middle of the night. I've yet to see him leave the table richer than when he arrived. At least he's no longer in physical danger when he loses!

Growing Up Leffler

Ido: Growing up in the Leffler household was anything but typical. We were a team. My brother and I, as I said, grew up fast and we were given a ton of responsibility very early. As a result, I never felt intimidated by anyone or anything; my parents never had situations that were "adult only." They always invited us to be a part of the conversation, and they always gave us the same respect they gave to their peers.

As a result, we learned to respect the seriousness of the situation, and we weren't bratty around the people we were meeting. We also never learned to fear people on account of their stature and position in life. Because I was exposed to powerful and important people at a young age, I learned they were just like us, human. I never felt the need or even had a chance to feel awestruck or intimidated by them. I do the same thing today, treating everyone I meet with the same respect, whether that person is a CEO or just starting out on their working life.

At Yes To, I ask all our high-powered guests to spend fifteen minutes with the team whenever possible. I don't want to keep these connections for myself. I want my team to share in all the benefits of knowing the powerful and important people who come through our doors.

My parents' other big gift to us as kids — and I thank them for this every day — was instilling in each of us a passion for travel. Even at our darkest moments, when it looked like we'd be broke forever, my parents worked hard to figure out ways to make trips together and experience new and unfamiliar cultures. It helped that they believed travel was all about mingling with everyday people, rather than staying at high-end resorts. My brother and I spent big chunks of our youth on 747s heading for one unusual destination or another. The whole point of each trip was discovering new and exciting things, and that meant meeting the local people. Our travels allowed me to become quite worldly. In fact, I was so confident and comfortable in foreign situations that when I was eleven, I persuaded my parents to let me go to Israel on my own. I flew—alone—from Sydney to Bangkok to Athens and finally to Tel Aviv (more than thirty-six hours with connections!).

Now that I have kids, I wonder what the hell my parents were thinking! There's no way I'm letting my daughters fly around the world solo. But my parents had faith in my brother and I and encouraged this worldly approach to life. They always gave us as much independence as we could handle.

In my late teens, I took off on a backpacking trip through Asia, traveling on trains and buses and eschewing the tourist machinery. I almost froze to death on a night train through the desert, surviving only by crawling inside my backpack to sleep, and was press-ganged into an impromptu international cricket team in Pushkar, Rajasthan (we were a motley crew of Anglo tourists who were quickly trounced by the Rajasthani pros).

Along the way I broke bread with the poorest of the poor, who invited me into their homes with warmth and grace and love. I learned that you can have faith in your fellow man, and that if you find yourself starving on a nineteen-hour train ride through the Indian countryside, someone will offer you a chapati,* a hot tea, and a smile, even if they are so poor that that's literally all they have. There's less to be afraid of out there than we think.

Today as a businessman I still believe that the most important gifts you can give someone—be it your kids or an employee—are autonomy, a sense of fearlessness about the world, and the belief that they can make a difference. My coworkers at Yes To know that we have faith in them. We believe they are capable of doing the work that we have hired them to do. We want them to feel fully empowered to run their slice of the company without the feeling that we are hovering

---

* traditional Indian bread

over them. As a result, they feel a sense of ownership. Our baby is their baby too.

The Value of Believing in Yourself

Lance: One of my formative experiences in becoming an entrepreneur was spending recesses with a classmate of mine, Brett Levy. Brett was a few years ahead of me in school. When I first met him, he was just another snotty kid in a school uniform, but today he's the mastermind behind the biggest prepaid mobile airtime distribution company in Africa, with operations in Mexico and India. He is also one of South Africa's most successful entrepreneurs under forty.

As a kid, Brett was always nice and friendly, but he also had a cheeky kind of arrogance and an aura of confidence that a lot of entrepreneurs emit; you want to be around them, and in turn they draw people into their space.

For all his popularity, Brett was also my arch-nemesis for the simple reason that he was the all-time reigning champ at the most popular game in school: Garbage Pail Kids.

Garbage Pail Kids were collectable cards that became one of those fads that tear through a school for a few months. South African kids weren't interested in baseball—let's be honest, cricket is far superior—so instead of trading baseball cards, we traded GPKs. The cards also helped identify the gamblers, the risk-takers, and the most aggressive mini-businessmen in the playground.

Garbage Pail Kids was a risk-taker's game. You'd place your cards face down, challenge a friend to do the same, and then slap the cards till they flipped over. He whose cards flipped first won. It was a high-risk, high-reward game I felt I could crack; naturally, I loved it.

The only problem was, I sucked. I always lost. I had the brain-power, but my nine-year-old hands just couldn't hit the ground hard enough to make the cards turn over.

Brett Levy played with the highest stakes in the schoolyard; instead of putting one card down, he would challenge people to thirty. Kids would lose their entire worldly fortunes to Brett in one round, and he'd triumphantly throw their cards in his lunch box with all his other winnings.

Being an entrepreneur is all about playing the odds, because you never have enough time or data to make a completely informed decision. You have to be OK with making 80 percent of your decisions while seeing only 20 percent of the picture. Brett may have played a reckless game, but he had certain qualities that I've seen in every other successful entrepreneur since I left the playground: He was arrogant and willing to take risks. He had confidence in his abilities and was willing to bet big on himself. He was eager to grow and turn his pack of twenty cards into two hundred.

If you're not a person with conviction, perfectly comfortable going with your gut, then you need to take the time to learn to hear what your gut is trying to say. Go do something scary, like BASE jumping.* Take a flying leap off a few buildings or a couple of bridges and you'll hear your gut loud and clear — that way, you'll know what to look out for in the future! The flip side of this is being able to accept when your gut instincts led you astray and having the resilience to let go of your mistake.

Brett also taught me that a great opportunity could still be all wrong for you. I wanted to win at Garbage Pail Kids. I knew I was as smart as or smarter than the other kids in the yard. I had the intelligence, the arrogance, and the risk tolerance, but I lacked the requisite dexterity to excel at the game. The most valuable lesson that came out of this experience was learning when to stop and walk away.

Since Yes To has taken off, I've heard lots of people who say: "I want to start a natural skin-care line and succeed, just like you guys

---

* Our lawyers: Don't actually go BASE jumping.

did." My response is, "Hang on there! Ido and I worked on seventy-five other brands before we got to the one that succeeded. We were able to look at the ideas that didn't work and say, 'I really wanted this to work, it sucks that it didn't, but that's OK,' and walk away from something that we really, really wanted to make happen."

Lessons from an International Background

Lance: As you've probably figured out by now, Ido and I had relatively unusual backgrounds, and we strongly believe that these formative experiences were crucial components of our present-day success. We were both shaped by the experience of growing up in exciting but relatively dangerous countries, and then emigrating to the more peaceful and predictable comforts of Australia. This gave each of us an edge. We are both very aware of what it's like to live in an uncertain world, where things could go very wrong, very quickly.

I experienced the sanctions against South Africa in the eighties, when almost all international imports were banned. If you wanted chewing gum, sneakers, or anything that wasn't complete rubbish, you'd have to smuggle it in yourself. The sanctions created a huge black-market economy. For kids, the most valuable items in that economy were toys and candy. For adults, it was information and opportunities from the outside world. The sanctions blocked almost everything from Europe or America. If you wanted to watch the Soccer World Cup, you'd have to wait until the local video store had Betamax copies of the matches. I've still never seen the soccer finals of the 1986 World Cup. Some jerk forgot to return the tape. I wonder if it's on YouTube . . .

Ido: We are both mongrels! I have the attitude of an Israeli and (luckily) the manners of an Australian, a calm and friendly exterior with a fiery "nothing can stop me" drive that is always trying to push the politeness aside. Sometimes at the flick of a switch. I can go from being a very cool, calm Anglo individual to being a wildly gesticulating Israeli very quickly. Both these aspects of my personality have been beneficial to me in business and in life; they allow me to function well within a traditional business environment and within the more explosive, impassioned, "no rules" start-up environment.

I am a huge believer in doing anything you can to get out there and experience other cultures, other ways of living and doing things. Not just as for fun, but also as a key to learning the kind of flexibility that will allow you to be comfortable in unfamiliar and challenging environments. I understand that most people don't have the opportunities that we did as kids. Still, even if you can't pick up and spend six months backpacking through Southeast Asia, force yourself to get out and experience "different" within your own world. Find the part of town where you are the outsider. Go to a restaurant where you are the only person not speaking the language and where you can't read the menu. The idea is to be a little uncomfortable and off-balance for a short period of time. We are all tempted to think that our experience of life is "normal," but this is incredibly limiting. There's a vast world (full of opportunity) out there that is nothing like our local environment. Force yourself to be on the outside looking in, and see what you can learn. Perhaps you are more flexible and adaptable than you realize?

Lance: As wonderful as life can be in Australia and the United States, you need to get out there and see how other cultures do things. In South Africa, we grew up with none of the first-world efficiencies I now take for granted. People were very smart, but you had to do things the hard way, and be very creative to get even basic things done. But back then no one knew if the political situation was going to stabilize or become more chaotic. Because of this we were always thinking about how to schlep money overseas.

To some extent, finagling the system was OK. The rules were very dotted, with plenty of leeway for a smooth talker and fast thinker.

Providing you didn't go over the line, you could take a few chances and bend a few regulations. There was, and still is, a culture of "pushing it," which is typical of any third-world country. People constantly test the rules to see what they can get away with, and that's OK. Because of this, South Africa is now a country of very aggressive and highly ambitious businesspeople.

A lot of third-worlders struggle to fit into the rigidity of the first-world way of doing things. They don't understand that rules in the first world are rigid and that you must follow them to a T. As an adult, I found it hard to work within the corporate world in Australia. My coworkers had grown up in a rigid system where they would be punished to the full extent of the law if they stepped outside the lines, whereas I'd come from a country where you could pay the equivalent of $200 for a government worker to burn your tax record.

By the mid-nineties, it was clear that we had to get out of South Africa. The country had become incredibly dangerous. We had security guards that followed us into our driveway to make sure that we got into the house without being mugged, kidnapped, or murdered.

My father realized that if we didn't make a move, my siblings would split up and end up living scattered all over the world. We'd traveled to Australia as a family before and loved it. It is very carefree and relaxed, with all the sun and the fun we loved about South Africa, without any of the violence and instability that were plaguing the country.

The Family That Stays Together Gets Paid Together

Ido: After the housing market crashed, my father was so depressed he could hardly move. After years of active work on building sites, he would sit all day, taking antidepressants, and stressing about our family's finances. My mum had suddenly been promoted from copilot to captain of our family. She realized that getting my dad back to health, both mentally and physically, was a bigger priority than finding money to replace our lost income. We would still be a family, even if we were broke, but we would be nothing at all without our dad.

She knew that his weight gain and lethargy were making his stress and anxiety worse. My dad needed to feel better physically before he could start thinking about working again. A friend of hers told her about a weight-loss plan from an American multilevel marketing company called Herbalife, and she signed up as a distributor. The plan worked, and a few months later Dad had lost most of the weight, and Mum had lost just enough to look gorgeous and feel much better.

My mum's friends and colleagues wanted to know how she'd lost the weight, and after she told them about Herbalife they were eager to try it for themselves. Within a month she'd earned $4,000.

When my dad saw her first month's profit, he realized that this company represented a huge opportunity for our family. After getting his accountant and lawyer to check it out, he joined my mum and never looked back, achieving success beyond their wildest dreams.

It was the start of my family's second life. Dad told us he was leaving and not coming home until he "got this done." For the next two years he went on the road, traveling to Japan, Turkey, Canada, anywhere in the world he could get a meeting. We were so broke when he started that sometimes he would synchronize his flights and meetings so he could sleep on the plane, saving on hotels. One time he went to a three-day conference in Los Angeles and slept in the train station. No one ever knew; he still had his impeccably tailored suits from his old life and an air of confidence that suggested he was already a success.

My parents' determination paid off; it turned out that their personal success losing weight with Herbalife made them the perfect salespeople for the product. And they did not rest until they'd sold the hell out of it (and which they still do exceptionally well to this day).

It's not enough to *want* to succeed. Entrepreneurs need a sense of urgency that comes from *having* to succeed. My parents had no safety net, which made them strong, aggressive, and committed to their growing business. Remember when I said my parents believed in giving their kids the gift of autonomy and independence? When they committed themselves to their Herbalife business, they sat my younger brother and me down and essentially said: "Over to you guys." I was sixteen at the time. In order to grow our new family business, my parents needed to work overseas. They trusted that my brother and I could take care of ourselves and live responsibly and safely. In fact, they had so much faith in us that my mum wrote a note to my school informing them I was allowed to write my own sick notes. Then they gave me guardianship over my brother so I could write sick notes for him as well!

Lance: Ido and I think that being an entrepreneur is pretty much the best thing you can do with your life, but the reality is, you can be brilliantly smart, wildly ambitious, and still not be perfectly suited to being an entrepreneur. My father was a fantastic surgeon. He was one of the leading ear, nose, and throat specialists in South Africa. And while we lived there he dabbled successfully in a few major investments too.

Once we came to Australia and he could no longer earn a large income as a doctor, my father decided to look for some investment opportunities. Unfortunately, he romanticized business after having seen many of his South African friends making far more money from far less demanding jobs than being a surgeon.

Living in Australia is three or four times more expensive than living in South Africa, so when we emigrated my father felt that generating more income was very important. After some deliberation, he decided to invest in a friend's retail electronics business.

My father is pretty much the smartest (and kindest) person I know, but he is no electronics geek. He is, however, trusting to a fault, so he quickly invested a large sum of money in this business. Now, in South Africa he could often say yes to a fairly risky opportunity because he knew that if he lost he could go into the surgery the next day and make it all back again. However, he didn't have a medical license in Australia and therefore couldn't practice as a surgeon.

In the end my father lost almost all his savings in this one investment. The compassion, empathy, and desire to "fix things" that made him a great doctor became his Achilles' heel when it came to doing business. His desire to help his friend was so strong that he overlooked the fact that his friend's business model was fatally flawed.

My father has a great sense of perspective; he always looks at things from a bigger perspective and never worries if one little detail goes awry. If anything went wrong, he'd stand back and say, "I've got my family and my health, and if this doesn't work I'm coming out of this more experienced. I'll just concentrate and work harder on something else." I love this sense of perspective, and I've used it throughout my journey as an entrepreneur. It's easy to be so aggressive about business that you lose sight of your humanity and your sense of empathy.

Despite my father's occasional failures as an entrepreneur or businessman, he is an outstanding human being, and I'm incredibly grateful to have had—firsthand—the lesson that your humanity is more important than any endeavor. His perspective gives him resilience and grace and allows him to recover from huge setbacks and still feel optimistic about life. He doesn't hide behind his failures and blame them on anyone but himself. Most important, he repeatedly discusses failures with the family in order to emphasize the lessons he learned so that we won't repeat them. He genuinely believes it is worth the whole experience if it helps prevent us from making the same mistake in the future.

After things went south, my wonderful mother went out, found a job, and went to work for the first time in her life. Her minimum-wage job didn't make a huge difference, financially, but she wanted to take a little bit of the burden off of my father's shoulders and show her complete support of and dedication to their partnership.

I have learned some of the most significant virtues of a successful partnership from watching how my parents pulled together, accepted their changed circumstances, and adjusted their lifestyle to match their new reality.

Ido: Both Lance and I watched our parents succeed, fail, then succeed again. The failures didn't diminish the core values or strength of our families. We weren't destroyed by them. Our respective sets of parents saw us as equal partners in our families. They communicated with us honestly. They showed us that success is great but that a strong and bonded family is greater — in fact, you can't have the former without the latter.

Before you start worrying about success, ask yourself: Do you have a strong, resilient, optimistic inner core? Do you have an intangible "something" that supports you and allows you to keep the faith through tough times? For us, this "something" is our families; for others, it might be personal or spiritual beliefs, or something else entirely. Either way, this sense of yourself, this faith in who you are and understanding of where you come from, serves as your foundation to build upon.

Your inner confidence and sense of yourself is the ultimate survival skill because it means that you are never fully defined by any one aspect of your life. It means that even if your business dream falls apart, you know deep down that you have the strength to recover and try again. We all mess up; but don't sit around and regret a failure. Accept that failure and tell yourself, "OK, that's done. Now I've got to get on with the next thing." You need to be able to make a big move, realize it isn't working, and let it go. People get into trouble when they feel like they can't move on from an idea that they've committed to and invested in. You need to be able to let go of a dream that didn't work and commit yourself to a new dream that might.

Our Fateful Meeting

Ido: I'm the first to admit that I don't have any particular ability at football, aka American soccer. I was usually smaller than most of the other guys, and I never had the skill to play in the glamorous positions, like striker. My role was always defense. Playing defense is like being the drummer in a band; you're the last one to get noticed by the girls, but at least you're still on stage.

Lance: In 1997, I was just starting to adjust to life in Australia. I had my priorities straight, so the first thing I wanted to do was find a local soccer league to join because I knew it was the best way to meet and befriend people. A fellow South African emigrant pointed me toward the Monash Football Club and I went down and asked if I could play.

It turned out that they had a match coming up in a few days and one of their players was in Indonesia.

"Why don't you sub in for him and we'll see how it goes?" the team manager suggested.

I was beyond excited; I decided that this one game was my chance to show the team that they needed me. I had visions of a great season and a whole bunch of new mates to go down to the pub with. That Saturday, I played in the match and I nailed it, scoring a winning goal in the final minutes. I was on an epic high until I opened the local paper the next day to see the headline: "Leffler scores winning goal." What the hell?

Apparently the journalist hadn't bothered to check the name of the goal-scoring player. As a result some tosser* had gotten credit for my win from a thousand miles away!

Ido: Lance was furious. Here's this jerk that he didn't even know getting all of his glory! Having come back from Indonesia ready to finish school, I'm at the local pub, where we all used to go on Wednesday evening, when I get a tap on my shoulder. Here's this tall, angry guy looming over me, and he says, "So you're the jerk who's taking all my glory." And that's how Lance and I officially met.

Lance: I was so mad. I'd had a day to get really steamed up about my stolen goal and I figured I'd have a good shout at the very least. I'm just glad I didn't punch him because as it turns out, this random, goal-thieving guy has been the best business partner, and best friend, I could have asked for.

Ido: We didn't click right away—that would take a few more years—but it proves you can meet the important people in your life in the most random ways.

Lance: I had always known that I would need a partner if I was going to go into business for myself. Being in business is like playing soccer; it's all based on thinking and working as a team. We both felt that we had things to add to and things to learn from each other. Together, we could deliver the whole package. We have very different personal interests and passions, and somehow our partnership ended up almost perfectly balanced.

University

Ido: By the time I left school I was already a committed businessman; I have always loved working. I don't just mean high-level, first-class, business-tycoon working. I love being part of any really well-run en-

---

* wanker, pratt, jerk

terprise that is so good that customers come back again and again. When I was in school, I spent Saturdays working at a takeaway shop called Psycho Chicken. Psycho Chicken was run by a Greek family. The food was delicious, the staff was happy, the floor was so clean we could have served dinner on it, and most important, as soon as you walked in the door, you could feel how sincere that family was. Our customers loved us because they sensed how much we loved the business, and of course the core product was delicious.

During that time I also set up my own first real business, The Roving Bakery. My best friend, Evan, and I would deliver freshly baked bagels and croissants to people's houses on Sunday mornings. It meant taking orders on Thursday via phone or fax (these were the days before high-speed Internet), waking up at 4 a.m. on Sunday to prep the delivered baked goods in my parents' garage, and get them delivered by nine. Did I mention we were usually hung over? (Also, apologies to my brother, Itai, for all the 4 a.m. pots-and-pans wake-up calls!) It was a small but very fun business, and it taught both of us that if you want success, you need to be consistent, brand yourself in everything that you do, and do whatever is necessary to get noticed. We even managed to make local headlines for the biggest challah delivery of all time.

Randomly enough Evan now runs a hugely successful data storage company — specializing in deliveries.

After I graduated, I decided to spend a few years working as a Herbalife distributor with my parents, moving first to Indonesia and then to India. My experience in Indonesia was my first real taste of entrepreneurship and business building. I was given very few rules and no real guidance other than to operate with integrity and honesty and to "figure out what's going to work and do it!"

In Indonesia, I lived in a communal-living house called a *kost*. Meanwhile, I was trying to wine, dine, and generally impress potential business partners and clients in Jakarta. Obviously I couldn't invite them back to the kost; their kids or assistants lived in kosts and they would be less than impressed to find out that I did too. Instead, I would befriend some other very important people in Jakarta: the concierges, doormen, waiters, and bellhops of the Shangri-La Hotel.

I quickly got into the routine of finding a quiet table in the lobby, ordering a coffee, chatting with the staff, and generally being the nicest, least demanding, and best-tipping person in the hotel. Eventually, the receptionist would very sweetly direct my incoming appointments to where I was sitting. The people I met with made the natural assumption that I was a serious high roller staying at the best hotel in town. They would never have guessed that I was actually living on the wrong side of the tracks like a complete hippie. It's the little things that make a big difference.

The hotel trick isn't the newest one in the book, so if you're going to do it, do it right. I still keep a book with the name of the concierge of every hotel I've ever stayed in. I note down any details about the concierge's life that I can glean. Ditto for the doormen and the bartenders. The end result is that I'm generally treated like a much more important guest than I actually am!

The more successful you become, the less you need to worry about the external trappings. At this stage in my career, I could probably get away with having meetings in a kost; it would be seen as just part of my slightly unconventional persona and provide a funny story for the people I'm meeting with to share back home. Sometimes, when you have everything to lose, *appearing* not to care can be your strongest hand. Being blasé about having coffee in a hotel lobby instead of a fancy office, or meeting at a locals-only lunch spot, suggests that you are further along than you really are. People perceive that you've passed the stage where you have anything to prove, and they assume you are much further along in your career or your business than you actually are. It's a tricky line, but with enough confidence you can walk it.

After two years of successfully building my Herbalife distributor network in Indonesia, and two more in India, I decided to try China. However, right as I was wrapping up my work in Mumbai, the Chinese laws changed and I realized it would be very difficult for me to live, work, and make money in Beijing. So, after consulting with my parents, I decided to go back to school and study for a master's of law (I subsequently found out that my parents didn't see eye-to-eye on this decision; Mum wanted me to pursue a safe career in law and Dad wanted me to pursue the world of business).

Why law? In my heart of hearts I knew I was never going to be a lawyer, but once I'd been accepted to law school I decided that it seemed like the kind of smart, sensible decision a young guy who'd experienced a bit of success would make. This is one of the only times in my life that I tried to force myself into a situation that clearly wasn't right for me and went against my gut instincts. I was already addicted to being out in the business world; by that point, there was no way I would sit in a classroom for another four years.

I'd done pretty well in Asia, making a lot of contacts and learning all about how to launch internationally. I decided that rather than have a side job to pay for my law degree, I might as well start a business. I was in my mid-twenties, so it wasn't like I was a spring chicken, but I conned myself into believing that I could study hard *and* build a business at the same time.

Through friends, my parents had heard about a Serbian businessman named Dan who was making a killing selling an ovulation testing kit called Maybe Baby. We shook hands and the next day I set up a company called Trendtrade International; the day after that I was on a plane with a suitcase full of kits.

I had convinced Dan that I could build his business in China,

South Africa, Israel, and Canada, and this trip was my first of many round-the-world sales trips. My main sales technique at the time involved talking my way into offices to get meetings with people who had no idea who I was or why they should care. I knew that once I could get a meeting with a retailer or distributor, I would make sales. I believed a thousand percent in Maybe Baby and my enthusiasm was so intense you could practically feel it radiating off my skin.

However, in all the excitement I forgot that I'd already missed the first two weeks of law school. When I got back to Sydney, I walked into the dean of law's office to explain why I'd missed my classes. After all, I'd invested a lot of effort into getting into law school. It was kind of a big deal. We sat down and I told him about the business and what I'd achieved while I was away.

"Ido," he told me, "I don't think the law is for you. I think you should go out and do what you're passionate about."

The dean had an insight into my nature that I'd temporarily forgotten in my rush to apologize. He was 100 percent right. I'm a guy who needs to feel passionate about what he's doing, and my passion has never been for reviewing documents. I am passionate about being on the ground, hustling, making friends, and earning sales. I would have been a great but very miserable lawyer. Thank God I was smart enough to accept the dean's advice.

I know what I'm good at, and I know what I'm rubbish at. My biggest talent is that I know people — the second I shake someone's hand, I know what my relationship with that person is going to be for the duration of our relationship. I can feel the vibration in the person just off of a hug.

My second talent is that I know how to express myself, and I'm not embarrassed or ashamed to do so. Everything else I'm just OK at, and some things I'm really terrible at. I have very little time for the things I'm not good at, and I'm bad at focusing on them. Do not ask me to create profit-and-loss statements or financial forecasts. I can read them, I can understand them, but I am ridiculously terrible at generating them.

The more I thought about my future, the more I realized that working as a corporate employee, especially at a law firm, wasn't my path. It actually felt *more* risky to work for someone else and to apply his or her decisions, beliefs, and ideas to my own life. I didn't want my future to be in anyone else's hands. I decided that anything I did from that point on would move me in an independent, entrepreneurial direction. I wasn't going to be the guy behind the scenes; I was going to be the guy writing the script.

At that point, I already had a business and marketing degree. Looking back, the best thing that came out of my undergraduate degree was the diploma hanging in my parents' hallway; I don't think I learned anything I wouldn't have figured out on my own anyway.

OK, I'll take that back: One incredibly valuable thing I picked up at school was the importance of being a human being, not a robot, in a presentation. This might sound obvious, but at the time I felt a certain pressure to rein myself in and conform to traditional expectations of how a businessperson speaks, acts, and thinks. My biggest natural gift is free, clear, and very enthusiastic communication, but I wasn't always certain that this was OK. The practice runs that I went through in various classroom team exercises made me realize that the single most valuable thing I could bring to any negotiation, product development, or entrepreneurial endeavor was myself, my personality. Only one caveat: Left to my own devices, I'm like a kid trying to ride a seesaw by himself. When my strengths are in play, I'm flying high, but when it's time to crunch numbers or make forecasts, I'm stuck. It was clear to me that from here on out I needed a fantastic partner to sit on the other end of the seesaw.

Lance: I dropped out of law school after two weeks as well. Unlike Ido, however, I managed to actually attend a class before making that decision. Our first textbook contained a few hundred pages of plodding essays about the history of Australia's legal system. After flipping through it, I turned to the guy sitting next to me.

"That's a lot of reading for a semester!"

"That's not for this semester," he replied. "That's for this week."

I thought about how hard it was for me to focus long enough to read the back of a cereal box and decided to go into business studies instead.

The moral of the story: Know what you're good at and what you have a passion for. Don't try to force yourself to do something for a living that you're either no good at or that you take no joy in. Be a lawyer if you love the minutiae of contracts and having stand-up fights in courtrooms. If you don't, find something else to do.

After I graduated, I decided to go work for the biggest professional-services firm I could persuade to hire me. I wanted to learn, and I wanted to learn fast, so I ended up working for a global financial firm, PricewaterhouseCoopers, as a financial analyst. This was a useful experience at first. I got a crash course in all different types of businesses and developed a good understanding of how to analyze financial statements. I started to develop my own filter to distinguish good opportunities from bad and to spot all the elements of what does and doesn't make a decent business. I also learned a lot about professional corporate etiquette and the discipline that is required to succeed.

After about two months, however, I started to feel stifled. My instincts were to do things the South African way, which meant searching for opportunities regardless of my junior position, developing connections with people I found interesting, and then leveraging those connections. I wasn't going to sit and wait for the phone to ring in my office (a corner desk with no window). My managers at PwC didn't encourage this kind of "creative" thinking. Big professional-services firms operate in an incredibly regimented way — they have almost a high school mentality. There is a strict social and professional hierarchy and a set-in-stone reward system. If you do what you're supposed to do, you will advance, and if you don't, you will fail. Partners who are OK with this arrangement settle into the monotonous comfort of doing business with all the rules and rewards clearly prescribed and implemented.

In truth, by about 9:13 a.m. on my first day I'd realized that PwC wasn't a good fit for me, and I was in conflict with the partners from that point on. At the same time, I didn't have a clear picture of another path to success. I decided to hunker down, absorb everything of value I could, and slowly formulate a plan of escape.

If you find yourself in this kind of corporate environment, learn all you can. Lots of entrepreneurs like to say they are great at thinking "outside of the box." But we've rewritten the cliché to reflect our own beliefs. I believe you have to learn what's in the box before you try thinking outside of it.

Ido: I believe in constructing your own box.

Lance: A budding entrepreneur will learn everything there is to learn from a role at a traditional financial corporation in about two years. I believe that if you stay longer than that, these very corporate and hierarchical places will start to close down your creative thinking and ultimately turn you away from any kind of entrepreneurial path. So stay, but don't stay too long.

There's a reason why people spend their whole lives trying to know themselves: Knowing yourself is really hard. Both of us had moments when it took another person to point out that we were on the wrong path. If someone tells you that you're doing the wrong thing with your life, and that person has brains and intuition, listen up. They may — at least in that moment — be able to see you better than you can see yourself.

2

Time to Ride

B Y OUR MID-TWENTIES, WE WERE each starting to think about our next steps. We didn't know *what* we wanted to do yet, but we each instinctively knew that the first step was to get out into the business world and gather contacts, ideas, resources, and inspiration. This is a transitional stage in the life of the entrepreneur: You are laying the groundwork for your future, even though you're not completely sure what that future looks like. People hit this stage at different points in their lives. You might be a kid, just out of school, or you might be in a much later stage of life, perhaps after retiring from a conventional job, when the urge to build something new strikes you. It doesn't really matter. Being an entrepreneur is a state of mind, unique for every individual. As a wise man once said, "When you get there is when you get there."

(**Ido:** I said that.)

This phase of your career will involve the most sustained and intense, hard work of your life. Why? Because you need to create enough momentum to get your idea out of your head, your ass off the couch, and your feet out the door. People will tell you that ideas are like babies. Forget that — your ideas are like boulders, and you need to push them uphill until they have enough momentum to roll down the other side. It's hard work.

Ido: At a certain point, I realized that the most fun I'd ever had was packing up a suitcase of Maybe Baby kits and flying around the world selling the product. A more "serious" career might have been sensible, but it wouldn't have been half as much fun. I decided that I wanted to build off of that experience, the only difference being that instead of making a little money, I wanted to make a lot.

I've always loved travel, and I recognized that my ability to move happily and easily between different cultures was a valuable skill. I am a salesman, it's what I do best, and it makes me really, really happy. Even better is finding a fantastic product that offers real value and makes people's lives better but is limited because — for whatever reason — the owners haven't been able to get it into wide release. That makes me want to get on a plane and sell the hell out of it. In short, I needed to find a product that I was enthusiastic enough about to pack into a suitcase and sell around the world.

There were great opportunities in the health and beauty marketplace and this seemed like a way to really make a difference in people's lives. Making a difference was as important to me as making lots of money. I didn't want to sell a pretty product to happy people in San Francisco whose manufacture was polluting rivers and destroying lives in Sichuan. I wanted to be successful with integrity, and not every industry lets you do that. I wanted my business to be fundamentally good.

For me, for a business to be good, it needed to do two things: improve people's lives in an immediate way — be a great product — and be successful enough to support a meaningful giving-back program. Even at this stage, with Yes To still a glimmer in my eye, I was laying out how our give-back program would be a fundamental part of our business model. (Thanks to my wife, Ronit, for actually figuring out how we could make that idea work.) If an idea couldn't be good, then I wouldn't pursue it. Ultimately, the beauty business offered the biggest opportunities to do something meaningful on the fastest timeline.

My experience with Maybe Baby showed me how a great product attacking an existing problem in an innovative way will have global appeal. I wasn't going to reinvent the wheel and try to develop my own products; instead, I wanted to build bigger opportunities for quality products already on the market. I decided that Trendtrade's mission would be to look for Australian beauty products that were either uniquely good or had some sort of quirky appeal that would translate to foreign markets.

Now, the one problem with this approach is that women buy the vast majority of beauty products and I am most definitely not a woman. I like women — I love women — and I have a one-in-a-million wife and two sweet and funny daughters. Do I always *understand* women? That's up for debate. Ask my wife. At least I had the self-awareness to realize that I needed to know a lot more about my potential customer base and that I wasn't going to figure it out on my own.

So after a deep and revealing conversation about brands and products (over a few martinis) with some female friends of mine in my tiny cubicle of an office in Sydney, I decided that the next brand I should focus on was an Australian hair-styling product called Fudge.

I was very well acquainted with Fudge. When I was a thirteen-year-old boy, I had a classic "Jewfro." I would go through a tub of Fudge every few weeks, trying to tame my unruly hair. Fudge had this incredibly strong fragrance that would attract bees if you sat still for too long. Now that my Jewfro is a distant memory, I thank God I no longer have to use Fudge, though of course it is possible that my present-day lack of hair and overuse of Fudge are connected. Fudge is an iconic Australian brand and an incredible product. When my focus group of female friends suggested I go after Fudge, I practically slapped my palm to my forehead.

"Oh my God," I thought. "Fudge is a market-leading product in Oz that no one outside of Australia has even heard of!"

There was only one potential issue: Fudge had no idea who I was or why they should care. They were (and still are) a huge Australian company, the kind of company that would employ a moat, if they could, to keep out random salespeople. At the very least, Fudge was a company whose assistants and secretaries are schooled in the art of hanging up, "please hold," and deftly deflecting cold calls. Like mine.

The Beginning of the Better Sales Technique

Human beings are great at imagining obstacles. Think about the steps you need to take to make your ideas come to life, those mental brick walls that you know are standing between you and what you need or want. How high are they, really? Short of start-up cash? Legend has it that Juicy Couture started with $200 and a roll of velour. Lacking connections? Make a call. This may sound simplistic, but the most useful solutions often are. Think about it: Everyone you need to know is sitting at the end of a phone line. Why not just pick up the phone and try to get a meeting?

Right then and there, I developed a highly innovative system for cold-calling people. (Of course, when I say "developed," I mean "made up as I went along.")

To begin, I found the name of the head of sales and marketing. Let's call him Bob. I also found the name of Bob's assistant. Let's call her Sarah. Sarah is the gatekeeper. Sarah was the one I'd have to convince I was worth talking to.

If you want to get something from somebody, such as a meeting or other opportunity, you have to be very polite, but you also have to direct the conversation in a way that puts you in the best possible light. The more I told Sarah about myself, the less likely I would be to get a meeting. After all, while I had plenty of ambition and ideas, I had no clients and no experience beyond my time with Herbalife and Maybe Baby.

I knew deep down that if I could get in the room with Bob, I'd be able to make a deal with Fudge. But if I just called up and gave Sarah the standard spiel, I'd never get through the door. So, while I couldn't lie, I had to make the truth as interesting as possible. Here's what I came up with:

Ring ring, ring ring . . .

Sarah: Hello, this is Mr. Smith's office. How can I help you?

Ido: Hi, Sarah. This is Ido Leffler. I'm the founder of Trendtrade, the international business development company, and I'm in Australia right now meeting with companies. I'm in town for only twenty-four hours and I really need to get in to see Bob before I leave again. It's about the international distribution issue for Fudge. Does he have any time tomorrow afternoon?

Sarah: Hmmm.

At this point, I was sweating bullets. I reckoned I'd have one chance to get through Sarah to make an appointment. I could practically hear her thoughts: She's wondering to herself if she needs to run this by Bob. She doesn't recognize my name, but I sound like the kind of person Bob would meet with. Bob is busy, but if she doesn't make the appointment now he might not get to see me at all, which might be a problem. She could tell me she'll call me back . . . but in the end she decides to make the appointment now and cancel later if she needs to. She'll run it by Bob when he's done with his two o'clock.

I pretty much launched Trendtrade with the "I'm in town for only one day" technique. (Once we'd built a name for ourselves, we no longer needed to do that, but as luck would have it our "round-the-world travel system" usually forced me to be in a city for less than twenty-four hours anyway!) It works because it implies urgency and hints at possible repercussions if an appointment isn't made. The technique works even better because of the second element: extreme politeness. I'm never the asshole, even when I feel perfectly justified in being one. I'm always calm and confident and friendly, and I never let any concern come through in my voice. My approach is, "I'd like a meeting, but it's more for Bob's benefit than mine. Honestly, I'm just as happy catching an earlier flight home." The end result is that Sarah feels urgency on her end to make the meeting, and a lack of urgency on *my* end, suggesting that this is more important for her than it is for me.

And that's how a nobody from nowhere gets a meeting with someone who, if asked, would have told Sarah, "Tell that idiot to forget about it!"

The Fudge(ing) Factor

All successful entrepreneurs have experienced a moment early in their careers when they had to persuade someone to take a risk and be first. First account, first client, first supplier — it doesn't matter. At some point in your initial meeting you'll be asked, probably directly, for some kind of evidence or assurance that you've done this before and that it worked.

It's a tricky moment. You need to be honest, yet you also need a way to present the truth in such a way that it inspires confidence.

I knew I had only a brief window of opportunity with Bob at Fudge. I'd talked my way in the door, but if he smelled bullshit, I'd be back out again before that door had a chance to close behind me.

When I entered the beautiful offices of a brand I'd admired my whole life, I felt somewhat amazed they were even letting me in. Bob turned out to be a classic Australian: big, friendly, and absolutely no-nonsense. He was clearly a little flummoxed, having no idea who I was, but I was on the schedule and he took the meeting. Soon, he was laughing and we were getting on well, but I could tell his clock was ticking and he had things to do. I needed to play my big hand.

"Look, Bob. I'm going to take on only five new brands this year, and I'm convinced that Fudge needs to be one of those brands. If we don't do it now, we're going to have to wait till next year."

This was true: I had decided I could handle five brands a year, but what Bob didn't know was that I had only one other company signed so far.

"I know that I can make this worthwhile for you," I said. "All I need is your blessing, a bit of time, and a box of product."

Bob mulled it over for a minute. I could see him running the potential pluses and minuses of taking me up on this opportunity now or saying, "Let's talk again in twelve months." All my hopes and ambitions for my business hung on his decision, but you wouldn't have been able to tell from my demeanor. On the outside I looked like I was wondering what was for dinner. On the inside I was praying that my forehead wasn't sweating.

Finally, Bob said: "Frankly, I have no idea if this is a good idea or not, but I'll give you one territory and let's see what happens. See what you can do for us in Indonesia and we'll talk further."

Brilliant! I was so happy and excited I felt like sweeping Bob into my arms and doing an impromptu tap dance down the hallway.

The first yes is the hardest yes you'll ever fight for because what you're really looking for is an act of faith from the person on the other side of the desk. Once you have that yes, the next yes and all the yeses after that will become progressively easier. Fudge wasn't my very first yes — Maybe Baby had that honor — but it was my first big yes. And it was the first yes that made me feel that my whole future was hanging on the answer.

Fudge sent me a box of product and, just like that, I was in business with a legitimately iconic brand. This gave me leverage to convince other companies to work with me. I hadn't actually *done* any real business with Fudge yet, but we were *in* business. We had an agreement. Keep in mind, my big selling pitch to Fudge was that I was going to take on only five companies a year to do this with. I had only two clients, but I was going to take *only* five!

I will always be grateful to Bob and Fudge for putting that faith in me. The first time you go out on your own with your big idea and someone says yes is like nothing else. Subsequently, I used my connection with Fudge to get a meeting with a very strong Australian beauty line called Natio. I was roughly 2.5 percent less nervous in the Natio meeting than I had been with Fudge, and I walked out with another yes.

I packed a suitcase full of hair gel and moisturizer and traveled to Israel to meet with distributors there. As I result, I got an introduction to a company called Dr. Fisher, which is like the Johnson & Johnson of Israel. Their head of distribution, an incredible woman named Dalia, said: "I believe in you. Why don't you bring Dr. Fisher to Oz?" Suddenly I had my third big yes. Instead of blank stares, I had voice mails. Instead of an empty inbox, I had e-mails. I was a single guy living on an airplane, running from place to place with nothing holding me down. I kept buying round-the-world tickets until it felt like my bedroom, office, entertainment center, and favorite café were all within the economy-class section of a Qantas 747.

It was one of the hardest, most work-intensive periods of my life, and I couldn't have been happier—until the moment I woke up and realized that this was getting too big for me.

Lance: Ido landed Fudge right around the same time I was getting sick and tired of working at PwC. I'd been working there for eighteen months when I reconnected with Ido on my lunch break. We ran into each other at a local mall, sat down, and started talking. After a couple of hours—that I got hell for when I got back to my desk—I felt more inspired by his energy and passion for his business than I'd been in months at PwC. I'd always wanted to travel and do something on a global scale, so hearing Ido talk about globetrotting around the world with a suitcase full of product was truly exciting. When we started to talk about what Ido needed in a partner—someone with great financial skills—I felt even more positive. I hadn't felt this excited since meeting my wife, Loren, just a few years earlier. We were planning to get married in a few months' time and we wanted to move to London. Ido was actively looking for ways to introduce his products to the European market. It was time to make the leap. By the time I'd finished lunch, I knew my life's path had just changed dramatically.

Ido: Trendtrade was six months old and it already had good momentum. Even though it was the early days, I had very grand visions of where I was going with the company. I was working out of a tiny office, and although my parents offered me plenty of support and assistance, it was basically just me. Bumping into Lance again felt like fate. It was the exact moment when I was starting to realize that I needed another set of hands if I wanted to take Trendtrade to the next level. I was (and am) great at jumping on planes, circling the globe, and getting people excited about products, but if I wanted to grow this thing exponentially, I needed someone to throw those balls to—someone I could trust to do the job right. I wasn't looking for an employee. I was looking for a partner, someone who would be in the trenches with me and be equally invested in making the business a success.

I'd always admired Lance's financial savvy, and as we talked I realized I needed someone who could bring traditional business acumen to Trendtrade. That way, I could do what I do best (get people excited and make sales) and Lance could do what he does best (make sure we had the cash flow, follow-through, and infrastructure to make good on those promises).

Since Lance was getting married and wanted to go live in England, he could take the brands to Europe. We had huge aspirations, and this was an obvious and exciting next step.

Lance: I'd learned a ton of old-school "how to do business" rules at

PwC that turned out to be invaluable. Even the most innovative company needs to understand the basics of profit-and-loss statements and corporate ethics. But I knew that my days at PwC were numbered, and I'd even had a talk with my boss during which he essentially said that I would go only so far in the company because I "need to be an entrepreneur, not a planning services advisor."

Before Loren and I headed off to London, I needed a crash course in Ido's particular magic. I knew that while I was in London I would be taking meetings where I needed to be the Ido of Trendtrade Europe. At PwC, I'd learned how to be a good junior analyst, which meant spending 99 percent of my time behind a computer and shutting the hell up in front of the clients and letting the partners do all the talking. Clearly, this wasn't going to work in my new life as an entrepreneur. On my last night in Sydney, Ido and I went down to our local pub, ordered two pints, and sat down.

"Right," Ido said. "It's time I let you in on a few secrets." He took a sip of his beer and continued, "You'd better write this down."

3

The Secret Formula

S OME PEOPLE ARE BORN SALESMEN, and some need to learn the art of the sale.

The following advice may sound simple. That's because getting complicated is not going to get you anywhere.

We go into every meeting with a long-term view. This person might not be in a position now to buy our products, but in a few years we may be a better fit. If we form a great relationship, don't pressure them, and make it enjoyable to deal with us, then we'll be in a good position to make something happen further down the line.

These are the top rules of making sales, the Ido way:*

You're not going out there to make a sale; you're going out there to make a friend.

Why do we feel this way?

It's simple; we've all been pressured into buying something we

---

* If you've ever had a meeting with us, please skip to the end of this chapter. No need to let you know all of our secrets!

didn't really want or that we later felt so conflicted about that we took no joy in it. It's the same in business. It isn't that hard to cajole, pressure, or manipulate another person into placing an order or making a deal. But that person will never want to do business with you again. This seems obvious, but it's a lesson that often gets forgotten in the hypercompetitive global market. The simplest thing you can do every day is to be the person that a client or buyer enjoys talking with. Treat your buyer or client as a friend and look out for their interests, even when they seem to be at odds with your own.

Ido once wrote an order for two million dollars' worth of Yes To products, which his gut instincts told him was about twice as much as the account could sell. Turns out we had to take a big return on the order. This was the first and last time he allowed an account to order more product than they really needed or was good for them.

Our first goal in a meeting is to make a new friend. It's never about going into an office, sitting down in front of a stranger, and hustling some sales.

- First, you make a friend;
- second, you get that friend interested in what you're doing; and
- third, you show them how what you're doing makes sense for them and their business.

Most meetings don't end with an immediate sale, and the most successful brands we had at Trendtrade were almost always those referred to us by people we'd met and not done any business with. For whatever reason, we hadn't been the right fit for the people we'd met with, but we'd hit it off, and they'd taken the time to connect us to a better opportunity. So don't go in with the intent to sell — go in with the intent to make a friend.

Which leads to the idea of trust.

Earn trust first, and then worry about making sales.

Trendtrade didn't develop, manufacture, or ship anything. We were really selling only two things: our instincts for sniffing out potentially market-leading brands and our integrity. From day one we focused on demonstrating that the people who worked with us could trust us. Our clients quickly learned that we never overpromised, and we always delivered.

Your customers need to know that they can trust you. The more you say, "You can trust me," the less they will. Trust is earned only by consistently proving you have their interests at heart. A little later on you'll read about a voluntary product withdrawal of Yes To that could have destroyed our company. Arguably we could have done less; it was a minute issue that never affected an end customer. It's possible we could even have looked the other way. But the fact that we dropped everything to fix the problem proved to our account that they could really trust us.

Know how to connect.

Lance: You don't create business by telling people, "I want to do business with you." You create business by creating relationships, and you do that by connecting with people. You have to find some kind of common factor between you and the other person. Once I've figured out what someone's interest is, I can throw some random knowledge into the conversation. There are some areas where I'm weak, but I'll always have something I can use to take the conversation from awkward to exciting. Once you have the other person feeling comfortable, you can start to build that bridge.

One of my most useful relationship bridges is sports. I spend a lot of time looking up sports results, and I in particular live, breathe, and think about soccer all the time. Soccer is the most international sport there is, and I know enough about it that I can nearly always steer the conversation to a team, location, match, or player that the other person might have strong feelings about. Even if sports are not your thing, or the person you are talking to is not particularly interested in sports, find something to be passionate about. People love people with passions they can relate to.

Know how to tell a story.

This is a big one for us. Everything—from making friends to earning trust—ties into storytelling. Know how to tell your story in a way that both intrigues your audience and makes them feel invested in the outcome. Even more important, make sure that you and your partner are always telling the same story.

Why? A story is easy to remember. A rambling spiel about who you are and why the other person should care is not. Give the person you are doing business with an easy way to remember who you are and what you are about. Give them a point of reference that they can incorporate into conversation when they talk about you to their coworkers or accounts.

Know how to get a meeting.

You've read about the "I'm in town for only one day" technique. Now, as an experiment in social psychology and business strategy, put down this book and make two cold calls to two dentists or two lawyers and ask each of their receptionists for an appointment tomorrow. Tell one receptionist that you are in town all week and tell the other that you're flying out on the redeye tomorrow night. See which office squeezes you in.

Select, produce, and distribute your products with complete integrity.

We have exceptionally good relationships with people because they trust us, and that trust is often built over a very short time because they can tell that we are bringing them only products that are market leaders. During the Trendtrade era, our motto was that we would work with only market leaders or products that were going to innovate the industry — and our clients knew this. They understood that we would represent only brands that we ourselves had faith in, and that any brand we represented would have been tried out by at least one, and probably both, of us, sometimes to our peril. (See "Sexinizer," later in this chapter.)

Always meet in person.

You can't fall in love unless you go on a date. It could be a five-minute coffee or a six-hour sunset cruise. This applies just as much to business as it does to your personal life. If you want to forge a meaningful connection, either with a good-looking stranger on Match.com or the buyer for a major retailer, you've got to meet them in person, shake their hand, and see if you fall in love.

It's far too easy to misconstrue another person's feelings over e-mail or text — how many times have you realized that you've inadvertently offended someone? — so keep communication as direct and immediate as possible. Whatever you do, don't rely on Skype. Have you ever ended a Skype call with butterflies in your stomach? It doesn't happen. You need to see that person face-to-face, give them a hug, and get a sense of whether you two have any interesting chemistry. It's the same in the business world. An e-mail means nothing, a call means something, but a meeting means everything. Couch surf, crash, fly out the same day. Just take the meeting.

Never leave voice mail.

We never leave voice mail. Does anyone even listen to it anymore? If you don't get the person on the phone, call again. Charm their assistant. Get yourself a meeting. Just show up. But don't be the guy on the other end of that dreaded blinking red light. There's nothing sadder than being the person who can't get a call returned, so don't put yourself in that position.

If you are going to sell a product, sell it with passion.

Don't half-ass things. If you really believe in what you're doing, do it properly. Especially when you're throwing yourself into a new product or endeavor. If you don't have the time or energy to make it work, don't do it. If there is a tiny voice in the back of your head saying, "This may seem like a good idea, but it's actually going to suck up huge amounts of your energy and end up being a waste of time," listen to it. If you find yourself holding back from fully committing, ask yourself why. Every businessperson has a story about how they started doing something they didn't really want to do and that, as a result, it didn't work.

A great idea can still be the wrong idea for you.

Wear a belt that matches your shoes.

Ido: Make an effort with your appearance. It took years of my nagging for Lance to learn to wear anything other than bad jeans or corporate drone wear. When we unpacked for our first big sales trip together, I discovered that Lance had brought a suit that (a) had a hole in the crotch and (b) was the wrong size. Lance was so corporatized that he couldn't wear smart, casual clothing. We practically had to stage an intervention to get him out of the sad, outdated clothes! Eventually, we came up with a rule: We would always wear jeans and a collared shirt. In order to be taken seriously by some of these companies, you need to stand out. You can't walk in looking like a junior associate. If you can't afford a good suit, then wear good jeans and a sports shirt. A poorly tailored suit in a bad fabric is the kiss of death. Burn it.

Keep your opinions to yourself.

Ido: One of the first things I taught Lance was, don't talk about politics. He has very strong political views, and when we first started he would start full-on political arguments with potential customers. Once I'd banned such "discussions," Lance switched to soccer as his preferred topic of discussion — specifically the glory and splendor of Manchester United. It's OK to banter, but it is not OK to sit with people for an hour and talk about how, up until the day you got married, you had a signed poster of David Beckham over your bed. Censor yourself!

Don't be the drunken fool at the table.

Let's just say we learned this the hard way. Follow the lead of your guest, and always order your drink after they have ordered theirs. If they order nonalcoholic, you order nonalcoholic. If they get a cocktail, you get a cocktail — just make sure it's something you can easily handle.

Know how to stage a business dinner or office meeting.

Do everything within your power to get a meeting at a restaurant rather than in their office. Who cares what it does to your expense account? Your chances of getting to know the "real" person increase exponentially when you remove them from their work environment.

There is an art to staging any kind of interaction with a potential business partner or client. If you end up having dinner with a group, then pay the most attention to the most important person in the room. Sometimes the least important person is an interesting girl or an amusing guy; don't go for the easy way out. Don't focus on the fun sales guy when it is the boring distributor you need to be talking to. If you're meeting in their conference room, make sure you get the seat looking into the office and that the person you're talking to ends up facing the view out the window. Learn how to remove distractions and also to make it harder for an assistant or coworker to steal their attention and distract them from your meeting.

Learn how to play off of your partner when you are making a sales pitch together.

Ido: Make sure you have eye contact with your partner in a meeting. I always sit in such a way that I can visually communicate with Lance, and vice versa. We now know each other well enough that we can give each other a look that signals we need to change our approach.

Taking an important meeting with your partner is like playing catch: You have to understand intuitively where your partner's head is throughout the meeting. Lance and I are great at this today, but it took time to settle into that groove. One nonnegotiable we've established is "the nod." No matter what either of us is really thinking in a meeting, we present a united front. It's critical that you agree with your partner even if it means you're in a massive fight the second you leave the meeting. Today, if Lance says, "The sky is green with a hint of orange," and I look outside and see that it's gray and raining, I'm not going to call him an idiot in front of a buyer. I'll just nod — and remember to sort it out later.

So nod, nod, nod your head and watch as the people you are meeting with pick up on it and start nodding themselves.

Build each other up.

Ido: Shout your partner's praises from the rooftops, no matter how frustrated or annoyed you might occasionally be with each other. When I'm in San Fran, I'm building Lance up, and when Lance is in Sydney, he's building me up. Don't overdo it, of course, but make sure that you are always positive, enthusiastic, and excited about your partner. When I'm in front of the media, I'll talk about how we were looking for a great person, and since we couldn't find one, we got Lance instead. People love that. They recognize that the humor signals how much I truly respect and admire him.

Be funny.

People want to do business with someone who is funny and makes doing business enjoyable. Don't be too serious. At the same time, recognize that humor can be misinterpreted by other cultures. It took us a long time to realize that people in the United States often don't get our Australian sarcasm and dry humor (we hope that by this stage of the book you are starting to!).

At the end of the meeting, ask, "Who else could I meet here?"

If you've got your foot in the door at a company, take the opportunity to meet as many people as possible. Leverage your meeting and use it to "go viral" within the organization. You are essentially being endorsed by the person you're meeting with — you are preapproved. As soon as you leave the building, write down every name and anything that will help you remember useful details about the various people you shook hands with.

Follow up!

Always send an e-mail follow-up within a few hours of the meeting, and always suggest a next step in the e-mail, preferably about the next meeting. Make sure any communication has an "action step." Suggest some follow-up dates in that e-mail, or outline what you will be doing next and when they can expect to receive samples, proposals, and so forth.

Don't get angry over e-mail.

Lance: I have a hot temper! Whenever I was upset by an e-mail, I'd respond in a very aggressive and angry way. Ten minutes later, I'd calm down, review what I'd just sent, and end up feeling like a complete idiot for sending it. A hasty response only exacerbates a bad situation.

Finally, Ido and I agreed that anytime I was incredibly angry, I'd write my e-mail, send it to him, and then wait until I'd calmed down. Ido became a filter for my angry e-mails. Inevitably, I calm down and never send the message on to the intended recipient.

Maintain your personal infrastructure.

What's your personal infrastructure? You're your infrastructure! This means staying physically and emotionally healthy through the stresses of life on the road. It means staying connected to the people you love and making sure you are eating well and getting enough sleep. Pack gym clothes and work out. No matter what happens, we both make time to catch up with our wives and kids on Skype when we are traveling. Stay connected to what matters — it's how you remember why you're doing this in the first place.

If you don't back up your data, you're a fool.

Ido: To this day, Lance refuses — because he is an idiot — to back up his computer. He is willing to lose all of his data because he refuses to back up his computer daily. There is nothing, *nothing*, worse than being thousands of miles from home with a computer that shows a blank screen where your documents should be. You don't realize how much you rely on your computer until it is gone. Take care of it. Don't be an idiot. Set up a remote backup that you can access from anywhere.

You may be under the impression that Trendtrade was an unqualified success. But if you're reading carefully, you'll know that one of our most important rules is, always tell a story, preferably a positive one.

The truth is, we made a ton of mistakes with Trendtrade. These mistakes aren't part of our official history, but for the sake of our entrepreneurial crash course, we're going to share some of them with you now.

By year two of Trendtrade, we were working with more than seventy products between the two of us. We were basically drowning—we didn't have the time to step back and critically evaluate how our business was functioning. Although Ido's initial instinct had been to start small, handling only five products, we couldn't resist signing other brands that seemed to have promise. The end result was that we were killing ourselves trying to give equal energy and commitment to all of our clients. We could sense that something wasn't gelling, but we didn't have the perspective we needed to figure out what was actually going wrong.

Finally, Dan, the Serbian Maybe Baby entrepreneur who at this point rented us the office next to his and who had become our unofficial chief morale officer, sat us down.

"Guys," he said, "you're spinning like monkeys. You should be trying to do a few things well, but instead you're just doing a lot of things badly." From Dan's perspective, we needed to focus on what was working and drop the stuff that was merely distracting.

Dan's words hit home with both of us. We realized that we'd agreed to work with brands that clearly had major issues, and that if we'd been thinking more clearly, we'd have seen some of these issues earlier.

Two of Trendtrade's Most Notorious Screw-ups

Do your homework, know what you're selling, and learn how it works (or doesn't, as the case may be).

Ido: I'd moved to Tel Aviv by this point and was living in that hub of excitement and technology at a time when everyone wanted to work with us. Viagra had recently hit the market with a huge amount of press. A friend of a friend who had an herbal Chinese version of Viagra approached us. According to him, his product was all natural, totally safe, and could be sold without a doctor's prescription. It was called Sexinizer, and he gave me a packet to test.

"Brilliant," I said. "I love it!"

"Mix a quarter of this in hot water, like a tea, and sip it." The man was a little vague about the ingredients and how they worked, but I was young and naïve, so I decided to try it. In fact, I opened the sachet, poured the whole thing into a shot glass of water, and chugged it like a shot of cheap tequila. I invited my then girlfriend over and, while I was waiting for her to arrive, started reading a history of Australia. Not the sexiest reading.

As I lay there, I started to feel hot and itchy. I could practically hear my heartbeat. A few minutes later, my blood pressure was through the roof and my head felt like it was going to explode. My face was glowing like a red traffic light.

There was no denying that the product was working. Turned out that it worked very, very well; I'll draw a veil over what happened next, but Sexinizer clearly had the intended effect, to an almost frightening degree. I figured that if we could get men to use it as directed —instead of taking quadruple the dose, like I did—we might have a winner on our hands.

The next day, I called the friend of a friend, told him what had happened, and agreed to do business with him. I sent a sample by FedEx to a distributor in Canada.

"Just follow the instructions," I reminded him.

The next day he called me up.

"Ido, I didn't follow the instructions," he said. "I thought you were going to kill me!" Now, this stuff tasted like poison, but he'd done the exact same thing I had done, ignoring the instructions and giving himself a massive overdose of the product.

We decided to sell the product in Canada, but when we got around to doing an analysis of the essential compounds in the product, it turned out the manufacturer was using a generic form of Viagra. Each sachet of "herbal" medicine had the potency of four Viagra pills. Yes, we could probably sell a ton of them (and I'm sure some other distributor eventually did), but clearly it was a potentially harmful product.

Naturally, we passed on that opportunity.

Be wary of fads. Don't take on products
that won't have longevity.

Lance: We looked for products that were getting lots of press on TV because that was a massive interest driver. One day, I saw an ad for a new product I'll call Mystery Mints. Mystery Mints were little balls you could put in your mouth to give you incredibly minty fresh breath.

Out of curiosity, I tried some and soon fell madly in love with the product. I was convinced it was going to be the next Wrigley's; they were that incredible. We contacted the company and they brought us in to look at opportunities. They also sent us a huge box of product, which I quickly started to eat my way through. All was good for a week, until I suddenly experienced a crippling stomachache.

It turns out that I'd been eating so many I had given myself a stomach ulcer. There was something in that product that worked well as a short-term thing, but it was just terrible if you ate it consistently over weeks or months. If I loved them so much that I ate enough to give myself an ulcer, it seemed likely that others would do the same.

Mystery Mints was another pass.

The Lessons of Screwing Up

Here's the transcript for a typical conversation about a new product between the two of us in our Trendtrade days:

INT. TRENDTRADE OFFICES—DAY

Ido runs in, clutching a new product to his chest.

IDO

Lance! Look at this product—it's brilliant! We can sell ten million of them in our sleep. The beauty editors are going to die when I tell them about it. It's Oprah time. This is it!

Lance looks at the product. It's an antiwrinkle cream made out of hummus, moonbeams, and pixie dust. The packaging promises that it's great for your skin and can safely be used to spackle walls and regrout your bathtub.

Lance punches away at his calculator.

LANCE

Sourcing hummus won't be a problem, but the futures market in pixie dust is going through the roof. The manufacturing costs will soar if we have a pixie-dust shipment delay. And moonbeams are hard to source in the quality and quantity we need. Yes, retailers and magazines will love this, we'll get tons of press, but we're going to have to sell more product than the manufacturer can possibly produce and it's going to be an impossible project.

End scene.

Lance: We look at building a business so differently. Ido looks at a genius idea and thinks about how excited the retailers and magazine editors will be and how many units we can sell. I look at what it's going to cost to produce it, the likelihood of successfully delivering the product, and what the return on investment will be on the whole project. Somehow, we meet in the middle, with Ido becoming more realistic and me becoming more optimistic.

My bottom line always involves the amount of time we spend on a product relative to the amount of return we can expect to see on it.

"Ido," I'll say, "we can spend 80 percent of our time on Product A and make $10,000 profit, or we can spend half our time on Product B and make $30,000. What do you prefer to do?"

The lesson here is focus: It's good to try a number of things, but at a certain point you've got to jump on a train going in one direction and stay on it.

My background is in finance, and one of the most fundamental things that experience taught me is that even the best, most carefully considered projection is little more than an educated guess. This is my end of the seesaw. Even though Ido is often frustrated by my pragmatism, I have to counterbalance his raw enthusiasm with realism. This is how I explained my philosophy, as handed down to me by my father, to Ido:

At some point in any new business, you're going to have to take your projections, crumple them up into a ball, and throw them out the window.*

Why? Because the majority of new projects will cost three times more than you project, take three times as long to get to market, and generate a third less revenue than you anticipated. To put it more formally:

The Kalish Rule of Three

1. Your costs will be three times more than anticipated.
2. It will take you three times longer to go to market than originally planned.

---

* Don't literally throw them out of a window. Just get really mad at the projections, swear at them, contemplate the imminent demise of your business, go out for some inappropriately early drinking, and ruminate on whether your spouse is going to leave you . . . before pulling yourself together and figuring out how you are going to salvage the situation.

3. You will generate two-thirds of the revenue you originally projected.

There is a good reason why more than 90 percent of start-ups fail in the first three years of doing business (there's that number again!). This is usually due to a lack of cash flow, which multiplies the negative effects of everything else going on in your business. The Kalish Rule of Three helps you stay as conservative as possible in the beginning stages of your business. If you take your initial forecast plan for the business, apply the Kalish Rule of Three, and find that the business can still survive, you know you have a strong enough business model to see you through all the inevitable bumps along the way. So you'd better be prepared, even though you may not incorporate the Kalish Rule of Three into your actual financial model.

As you'll see, the first six months of Yes To were extremely touch-and-go. When we first started selling to Walgreens, we realized that we'd dramatically overforecast sales, but because I'd implemented the Kalish Rule of Three, I was able to act expediently and make the critical changes we needed to ensure we would have enough leeway to fix things. After this initial period, Yes To accelerated, eventually exceeding our projections in a satisfying way.

I still fully believe that you need to at least run through the scenario of the Kalish Rule of Three at the start of any new endeavor. Look at it as a mental exercise: What would you do and how would you survive if things were significantly slower, more expensive, and less profitable than you expected?

4

Partnership

APARTNERSHIP IS A RELATIONSHIP, JUST like a marriage or a friendship. There are moments when you will feel completely frustrated with and annoyed by each other, and that's natural. If we had to sum up the primary source of conflict in our own partnership, it would be as follows:

> **Ido:** Mr. Do It Yesterday
> **Lance:** Mr. Maybe Tomorrow

We have very different philosophies about when things should be done; Lance is a natural and shameless procrastinator and Ido is ridiculously obsessed with doing things *right now*. This means that we occasionally drive each other completely insane, especially when any kind of deadline looms.

You'd think we'd have learned valuable life lessons from each other by now. Ido might have learned to chill out a bit and Lance might have learned to respond to e-mails the same day he gets them. But no, we're still driving each other completely nuts on a regular basis.

As Trendtrade grew, our partnership developed. We made mistakes, celebrated successes, and planned our next moves as a team.

Now, having a work associate is one thing, but having a partner is something else. When we started working together, we weren't truly partners. Sure, we had a contractual agreement and a mutual understanding about how we were going to work together and what our respective duties would be, but we weren't *partners*. You find out if you have a true partner only on the day you wake up and realize everything is falling apart. In the next chapter you'll hear about some of our "oh, crap" moments and how we handled them as partners.

We are huge believers in partnerships. Having a partner is far better than going it alone for a number of reasons, and here we are going to talk about some that have come out of our own partnership experience. The key is to remember that finding the right partner from the very beginning is the most important task of your new business. Choosing the wrong partner is worse than having no partner at all.

With a potential partner, there might be an instantaneous connection, or you might hate each other on first sight, only to fall in love once you start to understand each other better. You have to share values and have trust in the other person, even to the point where you'll accept their decisions when your gut instincts tell you they might be wrong.

When choosing a partner, remember that being friends is sometimes less relevant than being allies. Going into a partnership with a friend can be a great way to lose that friendship — and a lot of money. Approach your partnership like a marriage, and make sure that the other person shares your core values about the world.

There are boundaries in a good partnership. We know everything about each other's professional lives, but we don't get too caught up in each other's domestic lives.

Lance: As I see it, one of the keys to a successful partnership is making sure your life partner has a meaningful and respectful relationship with your business partner. Ido and I are fortunate enough to have wives who have supported our dreams and our unbridled op-

timism and enthusiasm through all the ups and downs of our journey. They gave up career aspirations of their own so that Ido and I
could pursue ours. They did this because each believed in her husband's abilities and because each also believed in her husband's business partner.

At the end of the day, if you're in a relationship, you are building a
business for the two of you. So make sure that your life partner is
fond of your business partner as well. The key to this is communication. Keep your life partner informed about your business all the
time. The ups and the downs. We have learned the hard way that trying to hide a business downturn from your spouse is virtually impossible. There is nothing worse than your business partner's wife giving
your wife a piece of bad news that you haven't shared with her yet!
Make sure you tell them everything, preferably the minute you walk
through the door—especially if she's going to be ticked off about it.
Delaying bad news only amplifies the effect.

Of course, it's possible to succeed by yourself, but it's more stressful
and a lot less fun than succeeding with a partner. A great partner will
be invigorated by your strengths and will help compensate for your
weaknesses at the same time. He or she will be your ally and confi-
dant when things are rough and the one person who truly shares your
joy when things go right. A great partner will know, almost telepath-
ically, when you're about to take a face-plant mid-presentation and
will know exactly what to say or do to get you back on course.

A while back, Scott Potter, the chairman of our board of directors
and our lead investor, was introducing us to a large room of his peers.
He turned around, looked at us, and crumpled up his notes.

"All you need to know," he said, pointing to Lance, "is he's numbers"
—and then pointing to Ido—"and he's pictures." Which basically
sums up why our partnership has worked so well. We each have our
unique skills. Lance has a deep understanding of the mechanics of

how a great business operates. Ido delivers presentations that would make the angels weep (and order lots of product). Together, we're two kids in perfect balance on a seesaw.

You could play around with a hundred different sporting metaphors to try and explain a great partnership. You could say that you need one striker and one defender, or that a great partnership is like a relay race, or like the Chicago Bulls in their heyday. But the only thing that truly matters is that you have someone on the end of the phone who cares as much as you do and will try just as hard as you are trying. Sometimes the best thing your partner does is remind you that you're not alone in this game.

Lance: We have now been partners for ten years. For seven of them we didn't live in the same country. Absence makes the heart grow fonder and, despite Ido's incredibly annoying personality, I've never gotten sick of him. When Ido goes into a meeting without me, he pitches me like I'm the Michael Jordan of business. This works surprisingly well since I'm not there to destroy the perception.

A partnership thrives when you have a little separation. It's crucial to have your own set of close friends and social lives so that you aren't living in each other's pockets. You need enough separation so that you can each do things a little differently. This enhances the way you work together and has been the key for our longevity. When we both lived in San Francisco we rarely socialized together. We made different friends and lived in different neighborhoods.

A great partnership feels like the two of you are in on something fantastic that no one else will ever fully understand; eventually, you develop a code language for all the ups and downs you experience. Our code word for "unbelievably, ridiculously awesome achievement in the face of certain disaster" is "Frank." "Frank" stands for Frank Lowy, the founder of Westfield Group (the owner of Westfield shopping centers) and an iconic Australian/Israeli figure who survived World War II to become a global megabusinessman and philanthropist. As young men we were determined to emulate him, and ever since "Frank" has been our code word for success achieved in the face of overwhelming odds. Whenever one of us does something amazing, he'll call the other and say, "Mate, today *I'm* Frank!"

All this leads to our Rule of Happy Partnerships:

LOVE YOUR PARTNER,

CARE FOR YOUR PARTNER, AND

NEVER CARRY STUFF IN YOUR SUITCASE FOR YOUR PARTNER.

Ido: I had finally wised up and realized my good looks weren't going to last forever. At the same time, I'd met Ronit, a beautiful, smart young woman who didn't take any shit from me, in Isreal. I was hooked, and a few months later it was time to fly back to Australia to meet her family.

Right before I left Israel for Sydney, Lance and his wife, Loren, asked me to bring something important back for Loren's father. I agreed but then completely forgot about the wrapped-up gift in my suitcase till two weeks later, when I was standing in the customs line at Melbourne airport.

Now, this was at the height of my mania for traveling strictly on round-the-world tickets. I'd flown from Tel Aviv to Hong Kong to L.A. to Mexico. My passport was full of stamps from dozens of such trips. In retrospect, I suppose my travel patterns might have seemed suspicious.

I walked up to the customs officer and put my bags down. He looked at my passport, looked at me, looked at my passport again, then looked at my bags.

"Sir," he said, "have you got anything you'd like to tell me about?"

At this point, I'm still smiling. A minute later, I've been led to a separate area, boxed in with retractable gates. The customs officer is so excited his hands are shaking as he's calling for backup on his walkie-talkie. Clearly, he has single-handedly captured the bastard child of Pablo Escobar and Courtney Love. The man is practically salivating at the thought of the piles of cocaine that are almost certainly in my bags. I can see "massive promotion" and "customs hero" written all over him.

He and his buddies proceeded to slice my bag open, looking for concealed items. The unconcealed items were mostly Ronit's lingerie, bikinis, and sundresses; the last stop had been a vacation in Mexico, and as we'd packed in our hotel, she had thrown most of her clothes into my bag before traveling home on a different ticket.

Clearly, I was not just a world-class drug smuggler but also a world-class *cross-dressing* drug smuggler.

Finally, they get to Lance and Loren's gift for her dad. It's a leather box wrapped in leather straps with no obvious use or purpose. At this point, I'm ready to kill Lance and Loren. Those bastards! I knew exactly what it was and how hard this was going to be to explain away. I put on my most reasonable voice.

"You're not opening the box."

"Yes, we are."

"Listen," I explained, "this stuff is called tefillin. It's a Jewish thing that you put on your head. They're incredibly expensive, and once you undo the stitches all the Hogwarts magic will vanish. You can't open it."

As usual, however, the magic words turned out to be: "I want to speak to a supervisor." After another hour, a blonde lady in a nice outfit walked in, took one look at the "contraband," and said, "That's tefillin. Leave him alone." And walked away.

Two minutes later, I walked out to meet my future brother-in-law, dripping with sweat, completely disheveled, and more frustrated and annoyed than I'd ever been in my life. I'm carrying my passport in my teeth and a dozen clear plastic bags overflowing with my girlfriend's underwear in my hands.

Thank God Ronit's family has a sense of humor! I shook hands with my future brother-in-law and silently vowed that I would never, ever carry anything for Lance again.

Lance and I learned a lot about each other during our days of traveling the globe together. Lance is chronically incapable of getting out of bed more than thirty minutes before an important breakfast meeting. Ido is equally incapable of recognizing this habit for the stroke of energy-saving brilliance that it is. Here are some of the more useful travel tips we've picked up along the way.

Lance and Ido's Guide to Successful International Business Travel

Learn the local language; just don't speak it around the locals.

There are lots of great reasons to be multilingual, but the main one is that being smart enough to know a few languages allows you to play very dumb at critical moments.

We are both multilingual: Ido speaks Hebrew and English and Lance speaks English, Hebrew, and Afrikaans. Now, neither of us is going to be writing any great novels in our second and third languages, but we can understand and express ourselves in them. Note that "understand" comes first.

Ido: When I started doing business in Israel, I quickly learned that I had a huge advantage if I was able to conduct my meetings in English. I'm more or less fluent in Hebrew, but no one else knew that. As far as they were concerned, I was Australian. Why should I speak Hebrew?

Hebrew is a fun language: It's loud, fiery, and passionate. Israelis talk with their mouths, eyes, hands, and feet. Everything from asking for directions to ordering lunch can be an emotional roller coaster.

The guy who makes your sandwich will be your new best friend, then your arch-nemesis. He loves your shirt, then he hates your politics, and suddenly it's three minutes later and you're walking out of the store with your falafel pita. We are an emotional people!

In a business meeting, I have the upper hand when I speak in English. I am instantly the more articulate one, and I can control the tempo of the conversation. People will naturally — if unconsciously — look to me to set the topics and lead the conversation. If I speak in Hebrew, I am at a disadvantage. I don't display the same humor or confidence. I am no longer the most interesting guy in the room.

Lance: I really wanted to fit in when I moved to Israel, but to speak Hebrew like a local was tough. My Hebrew eventually got better, but I definitely said yes to and smiled at a few things I really should have said no to, and vice versa.

Ido: Another advantage of not speaking the language is that it gets you out of traffic fines. We got pulled over outside of Tel Aviv.

"Do not in any shape or form speak Hebrew," I whispered to Lance. "We don't speak Hebrew." The cop asked for a license and I handed him my Australian one and told him in English that I'd arrived only three days ago. He looked at us, and I could tell he was thinking, "bullshit."

"I'm going to call this license into HQ and check it out," he said, "and if I find out that you have an Israeli license, you're going to spend the night in jail." He was speaking to me in Hebrew, but I answered in English.

"Israeli license?" I exclaimed. "What Israeli license? We're from Australia, mate!"

Suddenly I was sweating bullets. I'd been living in Tel Aviv for almost three years by that point and should have held an Israeli license. I looked at Lance and saw panic all over his face.

After ten minutes in his car, calling in my license, the cop walked back, grabbed my shoulder, and squeezed.

"So you *are* from Australia," he said. "I *love* Australia . . ." In that moment we were best friends, he let us off, and probably would have given us a police escort with sirens wailing if we'd asked. Once again, having a great accent, in this case Australian, always helps!

The same thing can be applied anywhere.

As we've pointed out before — and will point out again — there are huge benefits to being the odd kid, the guy who's a little different from everyone else. We are different because of our international background, but there are many ways to stand out in a positive way. Most people love diversity and crave hearing about the unique experiences of people from outside of their community. New York and London are ridiculously good fun because every time you go out, you can meet a new person from an unfamiliar country.

Lance: In Australia, I play the "born in Africa" card. I've got a list of stories that could happen only in South Africa, ranging from the time I almost got hijacked in Johannesburg to the one that ends with me almost being a lion's dinner while on safari.

The benefit of being the "different" guy is in the way it affects how other people react to you. People are always a little curious to know who you are and what you're doing. This smidgen of curiosity gives you an opening; you have a slightly better chance of making a connection and perhaps turning that connection to your advantage. Try to be the "different" person in any way you can. I'm always interested when I shake hands with someone who is not the person I imagined he or she would be. It makes me curious. I naturally want to know more.

Don't be afraid to be the outsider. Don't be afraid to speak a local language badly or mess up the grammar. Don't be afraid to look like an idiot occasionally. Never let your fear of looking stupid stop you from trying to communicate or forge new relationships or friendships.

The last time we were in Japan, we got kicked out of three small, locals-only restaurants in a row because we didn't speak Japanese.

When we finally found a place that allowed us to sit down, the waitresses ignored us until we started clucking and flapping "wings" to signify chicken. Only then were we able to catch a waitress's attention and order dinner!

On the minus side, there are three waitresses in Tokyo who think we are complete idiots, but on the plus, there is a fourth waitress who thinks we are complete idiots but will never forget us (and will probably remember our dinner order if we return).

Associate yourself with the airline and hotel brands that represent who you are or what you want your brand to be.

One of our business philosophies is that everything has to be on-brand because, as they say, perception is everything. This was especially true when we started out, and nobody knew—or cared—who we were. We needed to make the biggest impression we could on a modest budget. We wanted everything about us, from the way we dressed to the airline we flew, to tell a little part of our story. We quickly realized that we didn't necessarily have to be at the best hotel as long as it was the hotel that best represented our brand.

You meet a lot of people when you are making international business, so it makes your life a hell of a lot easier if you let the external trappings of your appearance, hotel, rental car, or airline do some of the talking for you. If you stay at the W hotel, that says something different than if you stay at the Four Seasons, and these little "tells" have to be actively managed when you are building a brand.

Ido's rule was that we always had to stay at funky, boutique hotels when we were first going out on the road with Trendtrade. We were working on a modest budget, so our choices were between blandly corporate and cheap or quirkily unpredictable and cheap. Since "bland and cheap" is too depressing for words, we picked "quirky and cheap" instead.

Sometimes our choices backfired.

Lance: I am very claustrophobic. The more flying I did, the worse it became. Eventually, it got so bad that I'd start having panic attacks anytime I flew for more than a couple of hours. Right at the beginning of Yes To, I had to get from Tel Aviv to Hong Kong to meet Ido for a big meeting.

The departure gate was packed with people pushing past each other to get on. I was sitting at the gate, doing my deep-breathing meditation exercises and saying, "I can do this!" over and over. We finally boarded, and I found my seat — all the way at the back of the plane, by the toilets. I sat down. It felt very hot.

"Hmm," I thought to myself. "These are tight walls." My knees were pressing against the back of the seat in front of me, there was a terrible smell, and we hadn't even taken off yet. I started scratching myself, but the more I scratched, the more my face itched. I started scratching at my face like a lunatic. Suddenly, I was overwhelmed with the fear of having a panic attack, which of course caused me to have an actual panic attack. I couldn't breathe, and it was so hot, and the guy next to me went, "Mate, just read this magazine and relax."

Ido: Lance had had a series of panic attacks on planes, and I was already worried he'd be certifiably crazy by the time he got to Hong Kong. He called me right before his scheduled takeoff, and said, "Ido, they had to escort me off the plane; you're going to have to do it by yourself, mate."

"What? Are you kidding me?"

"Ha, got you fooled," Lance said. "The flight attendants were so worried about me that I got upgraded to first class. Now I'm never getting off this plane."

Lance: A panic attack is a horrifying, debilitating experience; and to some level it was probably triggered by the stress of building our business coupled with anxiety about supporting my new family. This is the reality of life as an entrepreneur; you are under a huge amount of pressure from different areas of your life.

I arrived in Hong Kong feeling pretty good. I assumed that Ido had booked us a room in a nice hotel, one with lots of light and air. Everything would be OK. But, of course, the hotel was on-brand for us, which meant it was in an iffy neighborhood, had a lobby so dark you couldn't tell if it was chic or shoddy, and offered free "sparkling wine" at check-in.

I went upstairs feeling cautiously optimistic. I was done having panic attacks on that trip. I walked into a room small enough that I could touch both walls if I stretched out my arms.

"What the hell, Ido?" I thought. "This is smaller than my airplane seat." I turned around, almost tripping over my luggage, which took up half the room, and saw a window. I sighed with relief.

"As long as I have an open window," I decided, "everything will be OK."

I pulled back the shutters and discovered, to my horror, that the window was bricked up. My throat immediately closed, I broke out in a cold sweat, and I started having the panic attack to end all panic attacks. Thank goodness Ido arrived right after that and talked me back to sanity. More or less.

Learning to deal with the stress is key; lots of things help — exercise, diet, meditation — but the number one thing is the support of a friend, partner, or family member. And of course your physical surroundings can help soothe you, so stay on-brand, but don't let the cheap partner book all the hotels.

If you are traveling with a large amount of vitamins
in the form of a fine white powder, carry them in the
original dispenser, not a plain, plastic container.

Do we really need to explain this one? Let's just say it made for a complex and challenging afternoon trying to clear Jordanian customs and immigration.

Always carry a little token of your brand or
company as a "gift" or reminder.

A free sample is a billion times more effective than a business card. Everyone loves to get a gift, no matter how small. We have both received countless upgrades and perks simply by being friendly and generous to check-in agents and hotel receptionists. (Note: When we give someone a lip butter, we are promoting our brand and trying to recognize good service; we're not actively expecting an upgrade to first class. However, when you don't ask, you sometimes receive.)

If you can afford the cost or you have the frequent flyer points,
always upgrade to business or first class on long-haul flights.

Obvious, right? The cost of upgrading to business class has paid for itself a hundred times over. We've both sat next to (and extolled the benefits of our products to) heavy-hitting CEOs, celebrities, and world leaders. Business and first class (and the lounge at either end of your flight) are the best possible places to make useful contacts. Virgin wins a special prize for having on-board bars that allow for mingling mid-flight.

Look at it as an investment. It's like paying your way into expensive political dinners so you can dine with power players. The biggest difference is that in business class you still get the value of traveling somewhere, and you get to chat with your new friends for hours.

Lance: When flying first class, there is always a chance you'll sit next to someone's child or a random person, but the chance of sitting next to a "whale"* is equally good. My uncle, an accomplished businessman, was taking a thirteen-hour flight back to Australia after a trying, weeklong business trip in the United States. My uncle firmly believes in chatting to fellow travelers on these flights, but he was so

---

* bigwig, high roller, macher

tired that he simply popped a sleeping pill and went straight to sleep. He didn't even glance over to see who his neighbor was. After a long nap, breakfast, and a movie, successfully having avoided any contact with the person sitting next to him, he decided, with only thirty minutes of the trip to go, to be polite and say hello to the person in the next seat. It was Mel Gibson.

Find your airline and stick with it.

Have you ever been to the Virgin Atlantic Upper Class lounge in Heathrow? We have, and we're here to tell you that it is good — oh so blissfully, wonderfully good. Don't get us started on the gravlax appetizers, the champagne for breakfast, or the complementary manicures. Let's not discuss the ultraslick decor or the charming attendants. Or the private Jacuzzis. Or sitting next to Kate Moss at the bar. The world would be a better place if effortless and luxurious travel was a universal experience, but it isn't, and you need to do anything possible to become a one-percenter, at least between takeoff and landing.

We are both fanatical about miles, upgrades, and generally finagling the airlines' points system to our advantage. Let's face it: Long-haul travel in economy class has gone from tolerable to torturous over the last ten years. American Airlines has added a seat across on its 777s (going from nine seats to ten seats in every row), and I'm guessing United and Delta will follow soon.

So pick an airline and stick with it. Do everything within your power to accrue points. Despite our love for the groovy vibes of Virgin, we have now become committed fans of one of the legacy carriers, which is kind of like Virgin's boring maiden aunt. Very square but reasonably dependable. We made this choice not because there is anything in particular to love about this competitive carrier, but because Virgin doesn't offer the West Coast to Australia and Asia routes we need. Instead, we fly enough and spend enough on our airline credit cards to build up meaningful amounts of miles and in so doing boost our chances of an upgrade.

Pick an airline, stick with it, and learn how to milk it for all the perks you can.

By 2005, Trendtrade had reached a point where it was providing the two of us with a decent income and a certain amount of freedom. But we came to realize that there was a limit to how far we could go representing other people's brands. It was time to figure out our next step.

5

Yes Who?

F OR FOUR SOLID YEARS WE'D thrown ourselves into Trendtrade. Besides our families, our business was our sole focus in
life, and it was a fantastic experience. However, it became obvious
that Trendtrade was never going to get us to the level we wanted to
reach. When we started the company, the fact that we represented,
rather than owned, brands allowed us to expand our reach and diver-
sify our risk. If one product line didn't work out, we had enough other
irons in the fire that we could still have a good year. The flip side to
this was that we didn't see owner-sized returns on our efforts either.
We were also growing frustrated by our lack of control over how our
clients managed their businesses. They sometimes made choices that
either weakened or killed their brands.

Ido: When Lance and I went into business together, we had a
simple ambition. We wanted to be massive. Ridiculously huge. We
wanted to be the Richard Bransons of beauty.

Of course, this ambition came with disclaimers. We wanted to be
massive, but in a way that allowed our product to be natural and sustainable, our employees happy, and our impact on the planet negligi-
ble. This wasn't going to happen unless we were fully in control.

Lance: There is an element of serendipity in business, and Ido and I knew we wanted to evolve what we were doing. We wanted to be the machers,* not the guys working for the machers. But making that leap would require a pretty hefty amount of capital, and our pockets were empty. We'd invested all we had in our company (including the financial support of family to get us off the ground), and while it was self-sustaining, we didn't have the reserves to make any big moves. We decided to start actively looking for outside capital.

Business can be like dating. Sometimes you can picture that special person in your head before you've even met them. Other times, you have no idea what you're looking for. A few months after we decided to look for an investor, I was at a wedding in Sydney. Jewish weddings are tons of fun: There is always about twice as much food and drink as necessary and plenty of music and noise. I was sitting out a few dances when the guy next to me started up a conversation. Right off the bat I recognized a familiar accent and soon we were talking like we'd known each other for years. When the man introduced himself, I wanted to slap myself on the forehead. My new friend was a well-known businessman and investor, a fellow entrepreneur, and the kind of guy who gets a kick out of taking a chance on nobodies with big ideas. Like us. For the sake of the book, let's call him the Investor.

During our conversation, I stayed true to the rule and focused on making a friend first and not worrying about the business. I told him about Trendtrade, about what we were doing and all we hoped to accomplish. Even while I was playing it cool, I was aware that this was a once-in-a-lifetime opportunity. I desperately wanted to bring up the fact that we were looking for an investor. But I stuck to my guns and continued to confidently portray Trendtrade and Ido in the best light

---

* the man, the boss, George Clooney

possible. I could feel the end of the conversation coming. I had done my best to pitch the two of us in the most "un-pitchy" way possible by just sharing some stories and ideas.

Finally, the Investor remarked, "Well, it's too bad that it's too late to invest in your business. It sounds like something I would have been interested in."

Phew!

"Funny you should say that . . ."

By the end of our twenty-minute conversation, we had a meeting scheduled with the Investor on the other side of the world in two days' time. Ido was in Tel Aviv and I was in Sydney. We were both traveling around the world to see him, and that warranted a precisely scheduled, mid-morning coffee. He's that kind of a guy.

At the wedding, as the Investor got up to leave, he shook my hand.

"If you come and we don't do the deal," he said, "I'll pay for half of your tickets. If you come and we do a deal, there will be more than enough money to cover the cost of the airfare."

I've always admired him for offering to reimburse us for half the cost of airfare rather than the whole amount. His time was valuable, and he wanted to know that we had skin in the game. We had to be investing something in this, too. That way he'd know that we weren't just taking this meeting on a whim. As soon as the wedding was over, I called Ido.

Ido: My plane had just landed in Tel Aviv when Lance called me.

"Ido," he asked. "What are you doing on Wednesday?"

I had just met Ronit a few days earlier and I was already planning to spend every free moment with her for the next fifty years or so.

"Well," I said, "I'm probably taking this great girl out to dinner."

"Forget that," Lance snapped. "You're flying to meet me and our potential new investor. Pick up your dry cleaning, pack your Rolla-board, and kiss your new girlfriend goodbye!"

Eighteen hours later, we were hugging each other at the airport. Forty minutes after that, we were giving the pitch of our lives to one of the most impressive businessmen I've ever met.

As we got up to shake hands, the Investor said, "I don't know you guys at all, and I don't really understand your business, but I want to back your horse and I have a strong feeling your horse is about to bolt. Your business has been fantastic in helping other businesses grow, but the real value you have here is in connections, and it's time to put your time and effort towards creating your own brand."

Every business has its make-or-break moment, and this was one of ours. The Investor's support was invaluable; he injected enough cash to kick us into the next gear. He gave us both the capital to make a big move and, more important, the confidence to do it. His validation was the final push we needed. Now we simply needed to find the right product.

Yes To: Refining Your Idea

Ido: We knew we wanted to stay in health and beauty and to focus on a product that would be very positive. We wanted to create something that worked really well and made people happy. In short, our line, whatever it was going to be, had to have good vibes.

At this time I had just started dating Ronit and we were looking for ways to improve our health and appearance. I was going to yoga, eating organically, and generally living a super-healthy life during the day. On the flip side, I was still partying hard at night. I liked to drink and stay up late, and as a result, I no longer looked as young and fresh-faced as I once did. I needed some high-grade skin-care products, but at the same time I wasn't interested in using products with chemicals or additives. I wanted skin-care products that were all natural but would still work. I'd tried a few natural-beauty brands: Burt's Bees, Alba, and Jason, but they didn't speak to me. They were perfect for their consumers, but I was looking for something different.

Frankly, the big natural skin-care brands bored me. The way they presented themselves to the consumer felt complacent and predictable. They didn't interest me because they had no particular *need* to be interesting. They were targeting people who were already sold on the value of natural products and didn't need to be wooed. Their marketing and packaging said "crunchy," but here I was, a very noncrunchy person, eager to align myself with a natural-beauty brand and unable to find one that appealed to my sensibilities.

The more I thought about it, the more I realized there was a gap in the market for people who had green values but were living modern lives, people who were passionate about green living and sustainability but also wanted to reconcile that enthusiasm with living in the contemporary world. People like me and Lance, who wanted to have our carbon offsets and our first-class seats too. If we could create a brand that would appeal to eco-conscious consumers who didn't consider themselves particularly "green," we might be onto something.

Remember what Lance said about how business can be like dating, and how you never really know what that special someone will look like, or when they will turn up? In the case of Yes To, our business blind-dating and matchmaking took us back to Tel Aviv. We decided to take a bunch of meetings with manufacturers to see if there was a sustainable-minded, ethical manufacturer out there who could help us develop, formulate, and produce our own line of natural-beauty products.

No luck. Either the manufacturers had no interest in going "natural" or they had no interest in dealing in the very modest numbers we were considering.

I had one more manufacturer meeting scheduled before I had to jump on a plane and leave Tel Aviv for another business trip. I was tired, fed up, and dispirited about the lack of enthusiasm and energy we'd felt from the manufacturers we'd met with. It was a classic story: Nobody wanted to be the first person to take a chance, and our idea, "high-style, low-cost naturals," was too new for them to roll the dice on.

Feeling very low, I sat down for my final meeting with the owner of a skin-care manufacturing facility, and started going through my pitch. My eyes wandered around the room as I talked. The shelves were packed with various bottles and samples, none of which stood out until I got to a smaller shelf where six different products were lined up neatly. The bottles had an orange label with a large logo screaming "Yes To Carrots!"

I'd had an incredibly frustrating day, was in an annoyed mood (though I was hiding it pretty well), and here was this carrot product that seemed to be saying, "Cheer up! Be happy! What's wrong with you?" It was so loud and obnoxious that it was practically shaking my shoulders! I couldn't help it, my mouth slid into a smile, and then a laugh, and suddenly the frustrated, negative weight that was sitting in my gut lifted. How could I be angry when this product was so ridiculously happy?

I immediately realized that if this crudely designed product was interesting now, it could be something truly special if we really developed the brand.

Of course, I had to know how Uri had come up with the name. He explained that his retail accounts had been pestering him for years to come up with a beauty formulation that used carrots. He got so sick of saying no that one day he turned around and said, "I give up. Yes! Yes to carrots!" He liked the way that sounded, and a brand was born.

Yes To Carrots made me smile. I thought it had a funny name that was cute and charming but also clean and modern. If it made me — the experienced beauty brand consultant — stop and look, it would probably do the same for others. The original formulation wasn't particularly natural, but I knew we could change that to reflect our values and interests. In other words, even though Yes To wasn't perfect and was practically no more than a concept, I was ready to take it home to meet my parents — or at least Lance. Though it was the early days, and we hardly knew each other, in my heart I knew that Yes To Carrots could be "the one."

When I called Lance and told him we were going to start manufacturing and selling a beauty brand called Yes To Carrots, he said "there is no way" he would bet his future on a brand with such a stupid name. When he finally came around to it, he even suggested calling it Carrotonia. (I like to remind him of that occasionally.)

Lance: This was June 2006. As soon as Ido sent me the samples of Yes To Carrots, I knew we were onto something. It wasn't perfect — we needed to reformulate the products and change the marketing — but I could tell that this brand had something special. Before we signed on the dotted line, we showed the samples to our friends and aquaintainces and they loved them. Why? Because it was fun and quirky. There was something charming about the brand that created an emotional bond; it had a kind of scrappy upstart personality. People wanted to pick up the bottles and give them a hug.

We agreed that for the first six months of Yes To, Lance and I would split forces. I'd focus on building up the Yes To story and pivoting our business from brand consulting to brand owning. Lance would focus on our existing business, Trendtrade. This was important, since Trendtrade was paying the bills! I basically told Lance, "I'm leaving Trendtrade, mazel tov!"* And it wasn't until after the first meeting with Walgreens that Lance started to think Yes To might be real and not a joke after all.

Lance: Trendtrade represented six different brands, and like any investment portfolio, you had to have projects that pay the bills and

---

* Good luck! *Bonne chance!* Don't wait up!

projects that were "blue sky," so I focused on the projects that were shorter term and were making us money. After all, even the best and most revolutionary ideas aren't worth much if you can't finance them.

People ask us, "How do you start a consumer product brand?" all the time. They want to know whether it is better to build a brand from scratch, or is it more effective to acquire the rights to a brand or even just acquire the whole brand itself? It seems like a fairly straightforward question, but there isn't a straightforward answer.

After Ido discovered an early version of Yes To in Israel, we began to build the Yes To story and business. We had been working in the personal care and beauty industry for a couple of years through Trendtrade. Together we had developed a reputation for commercializing brands in the international market. We were therefore in a good position to make an agreement with the original owner and manufacturer of the Yes To brand. We decided to partner with him in a new venture that focused exclusively on the commercialization of the Yes To brand. We brought skills, network connections, resources, marketing capabilities, and especially *chutzpah* in return for his manufacturing capability and formulation experience.

Most people believe that it's best to come up with their own ideas and brands and then find a contract manufacturer (a factory that specializes in producing products for other brands) who is willing to develop and produce it for you. There are certainly advantages to going this route, but as with all business ventures, it has its major ups and downs as well. On the positive side you will be entitled to 100 percent of the ownership and control all aspects of the development of the brand. If you want to put that family emblem on the packaging or dragon's feet in the formula . . . go for it! It's your brand! But on the downside, the reality of starting from scratch is far more volatile and risky.

Developing a brand from the drawing board can be extremely costly (unless you own a factory!) and time-consuming. It also requires a ton of patience and good timing. You may have to launch without any reliable information and based on little but your gut instincts. It is an art, and there is a high level of failure. Look at the brands in your bathroom cabinet: Olay, Neutrogena, MAC, Kiehls, or Burt's Bees. Each one of these brands was acquired by a multinational company in search of its next big hit. These companies possess the ability to churn out new brands consistently, so why buy existing smaller brands? Even the largest consumer product players in the world are aware that it takes as much "art" as it does "science" to develop a brand that the market will not only like, but will love. They may be huge, but they still struggle to develop these types of brands internally. Multinational companies cannot afford to launch new brands that have a slow take up and small following. They are constantly on the lookout to acquire brands that have already "broken out of the mold" and achieved the elusive "art" factor that turns brands into cult brands, so that they can provide the science and resources (which they are much more consistent at) to take them into the mainstream. Therefore, brands that get it right straight from the drawing board are few and far between, meaning the risk of starting from scratch is extremely high.

Alternatively you can look to purchase or partner with existing brands that have already invested in the early development stage of a brand and might have some significant experience in the market, including customer feedback and market data. There are always manufacturers who are looking to partner with willing sales and marketing people, as there are inventors with great products and brand concepts who need assistance on the production and commercialization side of the business. Because most brands are next to impossible to value in their infancy, partnerships are often formed where complementary services are exchanged for a joint ownership in the brand, with equity based preferably on the dollar value of the services or resources being provided rather than on the current or perceived value of the brand in the market. So, for instance, it's simpler for one party to put into the venture all the brand's intellectual property costs (such as trademarks and copyright) at the value it cost them to pay for these services, and another party to put in an equal amount based either on an agreed amount of service hours or payment for upcoming expenses of the new venture. If both parties are contributing equally at the start of a joint venture, then both parties will be incentivized enough to enjoy the appreciation in future brand value. This will mitigate the unnecessary brand value argument that prevents many partnerships from commencing.

We were fortunate that we were working in the personal care industry and so immersed in brands that when we found Yes To we knew that we had found exactly what we were looking for. We also knew exactly what skills and resources we could offer in order to make it worthwhile for the manufacturer. Identify what your strengths and weaknesses are when developing a brand/company and seek out partners who can complement and help you take your brand/company to the next stage of commercialization in the most effective way possible.

---

10 things to look at and check off before buying or partnering with a brand. . .

1. Hire a decent lawyer! This is literally the first thing you do—it may sound "negative," but it is so damn critical. Taking over a brand is an intricate process; only a lawyer can fully advise and shield you against issues that may come up in the future. Don't sign anything without getting your lawyer to review and advise first! For most companies, this will be a "corporate attorney," though some intellectual property ("IP") attorneys might be able to help with licensing deals.

2. Whatever you do, don't procrastinate or try to save on lawyer's fees by deciding "we will sort it out later when we see that the brand is selling." Negotiate and sign a clear and uncomplicated contract that sets out who is putting what into the business with spe-

cific time lines and milestones, as well as termination and buy-out clauses (better to think through the "what-ifs" for worst-case scenarios, too). Identify the roles and responsibilities of each party post-transaction.

3. What's the value of a brand? How long is a piece of string? The value of a brand in its initial stages is almost impossible to determine. If the brand has some traction and sales through multiple retail stores, you can use trading multiples (revenue multiples or earnings ratios are the most common ones used) from equivalent industry publicly listed companies. But generally these are used to value only very mature brands in mass retail. Otherwise, just be sensible and base it on the actual sales and value metrics rather than "pie in the sky" sales projections of what it may be one day.

4. Clearly identify the countries that you will sell and manage the brand in, and define which countries or regions you are acquiring ownership for. Remember, every country around the world has different intellectual property rights laws, and you may run into lots of loopholes if you haven't stipulated which parts of the world are covered in your agreement.

5. Do a trademark search on the brand name and logo. In the U.S., you can do a preliminary search on the USPTO website (just Google it). You can do this yourself or more accurately through a lawyer, but if you don't, your brand can be doomed from the start! If the brand has already been trademarked, you can be prevented from selling any products bearing the brand's name in the future.

6. Ensure that the brand owner clearly and completely assigns all the intellectual property rights of the brand over to you or into the new venture. It's not sufficient to merely sign a contract that the manufacturer or brand owner will sell to only you, or that you will own all manufactured branded product in the future. You MUST make sure that you own the actual intellectual property rights of the brand (that may cover the logo, design, copyright, trademarks, etc.) outright and unequivocally.

7. Do some research to ensure that the person who says they own the brand and its intellectual property rights actually does own both the brand and the rights. A manufacturer might claim to own a

brand they exclusively manufacture when in fact they own only a license to produce it. Look on the USPTO site and identify who the actual owner of the brand's trademark is, and follow the trail from there. At the very least make sure you ask for some evidence pointing to complete ownership of the brand.

8. Do a comprehensive domain name and Internet search of the brand name. This can yield a fortune of information and also ensure that you don't end up paying a premium for your brand's domain name in the future. This can easily happen if a professional cyber squatter sees your brand in the stores and registers your domain name before you. There are plenty of them out there who are always looking to take advantage of these intellectual property loopholes. Once they own your brand's domain name, they have the right to then request any amount they want to sell it back to you. Trust us, we learnt this one the hard way!

9. Search online for information about the translation of the brand name in multiple languages. You don't want to end up like Mitsubishi, which named its new SUV the "Pajero" and started marketing it around the world only to find out shortly after its release that the name means "masturbator" in Spanish! Or the car manufacturer that created the "Nova" ("Doesn't go" in Spanish)—another stroke of brilliance.

10. Be ready to walk away from a deal if you are unable to agree on the terms you think you need (or if your gut tells you to walk away). Try to find a trusted friend or relative to give you balanced advice and to play devil's advocate. Let him or her push you to justify the deal and make sure you are doing it for the right reasons and not for the sake of just going into a business. Also, keep in mind that you can't do a good deal with a bad person.

And a bonus point . . . LOVE your brand with all your heart. If you don't love the look of it every time you glance its way, you will find it extremely hard to get anyone else to fall in love with it going forward!

6

Catching Your Wave

YOU CAN HAVE THE BEST idea in the world, but if the timing isn't right, you're up a creek. We'd sensed a growing interest in natural beauty during our Trendtrade days. Some brands were sincere about using natural ingredients, and others were clearly happy to slap a "natural" label on their product whether it warranted one or not.

At the time, nearly all the national magazines were dedicating space to the green movement, and some of the largest publications even had dedicated green issues. Blogs were just beginning to explode, with a significant number of them focusing on living a more natural, greener life. Bottom line, the green, natural trend was gaining momentum.

Natural and organic products were clearly more than a fad. They were becoming a strong trend. We looked at the rudimentary market statistics: The natural-beauty market had become the fastest-growing category of beauty, growing at an average of 8 percent per annum versus 2 percent to 3 percent for conventional beauty products. However, the natural-beauty market was relatively tiny at the time, meaning the big multinational companies didn't even bother taking notice of it. Most natural-beauty brands weren't even selling in mass retailers. It made us think back to just a couple of years earlier, when most people were busy dismissing organic produce and retailers such as Whole Foods as fads and niche players. As the trend to eat healthy, sustainably grown food gained momentum, however, prices came down and organic foods started to enter the mainstream retailers.

We have always believed that price is the greatest factor persuading mainstream consumers to substitute natural products for artificial ones. We weren't the first geniuses to work this out — but no one had gone down the mainstream route prior to us because they simply couldn't get the price of natural-beauty products down far enough to compete with the existing players.

Clearly, the only way to do this would be through the economies of scale achieved by selling in thousands of stores. Independent health food stores wouldn't cut it.

We had a little capital left over from our initial investment, a brand that had potential but needed tweaking, and a modest income from our Trendtrade business. The only thing that we had more than a little of was energy and enthusiasm. That we had in spades.

We figured we had two choices: We could be sensible, make small moves, see how they tested out, and eventually launch in a bigger way somewhere down the road. But if we'd done that, we could hardly have called our book *Get Big Fast and Do More Good*, could we?

The other option was to find that sweet spot where blind faith, quality product, and chutzpah intersect, and go for broke. By now you should be able to guess which option we took.

We wanted Yes To to be accessible. We wanted to build a genuine connection with customers. We wanted our brand to count. So one of the first things we did when we took over the existing concept was to tell a story. Yes To had originally been sold as a whimsical product. We needed to keep that humor but give it serious chops as an effective product and as a brand. From that moment on, Yes To was our baby and every day was a fight to get other people to take our baby seriously. Packaging, formulas, distribution: Everything was a battle.

We were selling a very big dream to people, and we had to learn to quickly filter out the ones who just didn't believe in or share our dream. It meant pushing a lot of doors down and pushing people harder than they had ever been pushed before. We were incredibly demanding of everyone involved, but the reward was that the energy of Yes To was contagious. People wanted to come onboard, and once we had you in our vortex, it was 100 percent go!

We quickly learned that sometimes it's more effective to go with smaller manufacturers who can provide you with faster service and are more invested in your long-term success. Go with companies who are brilliant and who have a really good reputation. They don't have to be the biggest or the most well known. Whatever you do, listen to your gut. Don't go with the person or supplier you are only 70 percent sure of. We made this mistake plenty of times — working with suppliers we didn't have complete confidence in — and as a result caused a lot of stress to the whole system when they failed to meet our standards and expectations.

Work with people who you trust and who you can build a long-term partnership with. The more their success is aligned with yours, the more committed they will be to making sure you succeed. I can't overemphasize how important this is. Make sure you partner with suppliers who are aligned with you — as soon as you are out of alignment, you are in a hole, and it takes a lot of work to get out of that hole. By "aligned," I mean that their philosophies mirror yours. If you are committed to being environmentally friendly, working with a company that doesn't care about pollution is only going to make you miserable.

We were both very serious about moving fast. Six months after spotting the brand, we were flying to Chicago to meet with Walgreens. The best way to describe that period would be to compare it to a very fast game of quidditch (the game in the Harry Potter books).

We could see the golden snitch, and we were flying as fast as we could after it, but we were also surrounded by people trying to knock us off of our broomsticks or casting spells, hoping we'd royally screw up. Every day for the first two years of Yes To we faced at least one significant obstacle, but that was balanced by our sheer bloody-minded determination to catch the snitch.

One mistake we made was underestimating just how much of a problem cash flow can be. It's a classic scenario: You get a few big orders, so you start to employ more people, buy more materials, and rent larger offices. Your fixed costs get higher but, as always happens, your debtors take their own sweet time to pay you. Apply the Kalish Rule of Three to your expectations for getting paid — it's going to take at least three times as long as you think. If something is wrong in the paperwork, you might not get paid for a very long time indeed. If you've forecast that you'll get paid in January but you don't see a check till June, you can get into a lot of trouble very quickly. Businesses live and die by cash flow, especially if they don't have access to outside cash. Sometimes you have to be more prudent than you want just to meet the needs of your cash flow. In the next chapter you'll hear about how we dealt with our cash-flow issues.

So, if we were going to go big, how big? We had tons of international connections from our brand consulting days. One of those connections knew a guy who knew a guy called Ralph. Ralph knew Walgreens. After another inspirational speech, we asked him if he would set up a meeting. A few weeks later, he called us back to say that he'd gotten us a thirty-minute meeting with the person responsible for business development in the beauty department at the leading drugstore retailer in the United States.

Now, we need to be really clear about one thing: We were moving at the speed of light here. Yes To was being sold in about ten outlets in Israel, and that was it. We had mock-ups of what the American version of the product would look like and not much else. The reality is that we had all the energy and ideas but were in no way prepared for the reality of building the necessary infrastructure. In fact, we had no real understanding of how long it would take to get the infrastructure up and running.

Ido: Moving this fast is a risk. However, I'd already met with various other distributors in Australia. They were beyond thrilled about Yes To, and I was bullish that we had something unique. I just needed to get a home run. Our unique selling point was our energy and our attitude; we were coming into a very serious category with something that was completely fun and didn't take itself too seriously. And of course we had me — a twenty-eight-year-old, ridiculously enthusiastic and passionate guy with a funny accent — making the pitch. People can sense a phony a mile away, and, frankly, the business world is full of phonies. When you truly believe in what you're doing with all your heart and soul and you know that what you're doing is special, then you're halfway there because people will recognize that honest passion and respond to it. We knew we were doing something special, and we believed that our faith in our brand would make up for our shortcomings.

We also had a solid tip that Walgreens was actively looking to put a natural-products shelf together. If we didn't act now, we'd miss a fantastic opportunity for Yes To. We were pretty sure that they were going to sell Burt's Bees as their primary natural offering. We were somewhat arrogantly looking to fill the number two spot. We were also aware that Walgreens might not look for more than three or four brands, total. If they locked in another brand or two, they would effectively be locking us out.

So, four months into our Yes To journey and a few weeks after phoning in my favor, I boarded a Continental flight to Newark and then Chicago. I had some mock-ups of our new packaging, samples of the product, and what I thought was a fantastic presentation. It was Hail Mary time. I had exactly half an hour with Michelle at

Walgreens, but the opportunity more than made up for the effort and expense.

I landed, checked into my hotel, and waited in the lobby for Ralph to pick me up. When he arrived, he took one look at my outfit and said, "You can't wear that to Walgreens!"

I don't wear ties. I'll wear one to a wedding or a funeral, but otherwise, forget it. I spent years working in the heat and humidity of Indonesia and India, where the idea of tightly wrapping your neck in silk was just crazy. I was wearing a very expensive suit, beautifully shiny shoes, a crisp shirt, and no tie. I thought I looked great.

"Ido," he said, "they won't even let us through the front door if you're not wearing a tie. I'm pulling up in front of Neiman Marcus, you're going in, you're buying the first tie you see, you're putting it on, and we are going to pray that we're on time. OK?"

We tore through the parking lot of the nearest mall like bank robbers on the run, slamming on the brakes outside of Neiman Marcus. I ran in, found the tie display, and *bam!* There, hanging right in front of me, was a beautiful carrot-colored tie. It had everything but a halo and an angel choir singing in the background. I'm not sure if the gods of chance concern themselves with things as trivial as men's clothing, but if they do, they were really looking out for me that day. I paid for the tie, ran out, and we were on our way.

By the time we reached Walgreens HQ, I was experiencing the worst pre-meeting nerves I'd ever had. I had no idea just how strong that gut-churning, bowel-moving, nausea-inducing feeling could be until I was sitting in Walgreens' cavernous and scantly decorated lobby. As I looked around, I could see people wearing name tags that said things like Procter & Gamble, Johnson & Johnson, and Coca-Cola. This was it. Sure, if I screwed up this meeting there would be other opportunities, but this was the World Series of chances; I just needed to hit the ball.

An assistant came and took us up to meet Michelle. I now know

Michelle to be a lovely, warmhearted, and funny woman, but at that moment I might as well have been meeting Margaret Thatcher. I was that intimidated.

As Michelle stood up to greet me, I felt something spark inside of me. She extended her hand and it came toward me in what seemed like slow motion. I thought of all the other guys in suits who had politely shaken that hand before launching into their presentations. How many of them had products on the shelves of Walgreens? I wondered if Michelle even remembered meeting them, let alone actually enjoyed doing business with them. I looked at the hand and in a split second realized that if Michelle thought of me as just another guy in a suit, my presentation was doomed. The only way we were going to do business was if we were friends, and the only way we were going to become friends was if she met the real and authentic Ido, not the corporate, hand-shaking, perfectly appropriate Ido.

The real Ido doesn't shake hands. I'm an emotional guy and I like to express that emotion. If you're my friend, I'm giving you a hug, every time.

I ignored her hand, stepped forward, wrapped my arms around her, and gave her a kiss on both cheeks: "This is how we do it in Israel!"

Michelle laughed at the unexpectedness of the hug; I could almost feel her trying to decide whether she liked my audacity or wanted to call security. Were we now lifelong friends, or would this go down as the most awkward physical interaction since George Bush gave Angela Merkel an unexpected back rub at the G8 Conference?

Michelle stepped back, looked into my eyes, laughed again, and said, "Good to meet you, too, Ido!" And we were off. She sat down and for the first thirty minutes of our half-hour meeting we talked about our lives. In that space of time we became friends, and it was only after forty minutes that she turned the conversation to business. This is something I do to this day when I'm meeting new people for Yes

To. I don't just jump in and start talking about our business. Instead, I make sure that I find out enough about you that we always have something to talk about beyond numbers and shipping dates. Frankly, I don't want to be in business with someone I don't relate to on a personal level. It just doesn't work. I got out my laptop and gave what I thought was a fantastic presentation. (Years later, it looks like a high school project to me.)

The presentation was very simple. It was about thirty slides long, and each slide had an image that I would touch on for a minute before moving on. There wasn't much detail. But there were lots of jokes and laughs. Each slide had a title that incorporated either a pun or a joke or something that would make the viewer smile. I kept my presentation focused but also loose; one of my skills is to know how to sound unrehearsed even when I've been writing a speech for months. I made a few jokes and injected a little humor wherever I could; I could be funny because I was also completely serious. I'd done my research. I knew the price points that Walgreens wanted to hit and I knew how Yes To could offer better value than our competitors could.

I still believe that that presentation was critical to where we are now. We didn't have a Plan B if Walgreens passed, because we both truly believed that Walgreens was the right partner to launch with. We had a dream to be a leading brand within their stores and we had to get them to believe the exact same thing.

From the beginning of our collaboration, Michelle, Lance, and I have been good friends and practically family.

We've always been curious to know what Michelle really thought of Ido after that first meeting, and writing this book gave us a chance to go back and ask her for the scoop. We love her answers, and we think she has a really useful perspective on how to connect with your prospective partners, especially in the early stages of your business:

Michelle: My first meeting with Ido was quite interesting. We spent a lot of time talking about the "naturals" industry, which was very, very young at that time, and why his products were different. Ido spoke with true wisdom and confidence about his brand and his mission to deliver best-in-class products within the industry. His stories about growing organic fruits and vegetables back in Israel and harvesting vitamins and minerals from the Dead Sea were show-stopping. He had me at hello!

Ido's passion for his products and how they would benefit our customers grabbed my attention. It was his genuine demeanor that interested me. He was deeply in love with his brand and truly wanted to share his products with all of America. It took me a second meeting to believe that Ido was for real. I absolutely loved the "fun factor" of his products, and how they were "good enough to eat"—in fact, I'm pretty sure Ido actually ate some product in one of our initial meetings. I also loved how Ido wanted to set up a "seed fund," which definitely helped me understand just how much he wanted to help the environment.

Plain and simple, Ido and Lance are just head over heels in love with their products—this makes all the difference in doing business with them. They are absolutely committed to creating partnerships with their retailers and they want the world to know how awesome their products are.

....

Ido: I'll admit, the hug was a hugely risky move. I don't recommend indiscriminate hugging as an everyday practice in your life or business. But I'm a good judge of character. I know pretty much in the first few seconds of interacting with someone whether we are going to be friends and whether that person has the kind of positive energy that will allow us to work well together. I sensed that kind of good humor in Michelle, gambled on my instincts, did something I felt she'd respond positively to, and it worked.

It's important to develop the instincts that allow you to read people quickly so that you can respond to them in an authentic way. Reading people isn't that hard. I always look first at how the person responds to my physical cues. For example, when you shake a person's hand, see how they respond. Do they squeeze back lightly or more firmly than you did? I tend to believe that if a person matches your squeeze strength, you have a winner, and if not, you need to put more work into building mutual trust. Also, pay attention and see if that person tries to make you smile. If they do, you're onto a good thing. Remember, a business relationship is still a relationship. The same general rules apply whether it's romantic, platonic, family, or business. If people give you those subtle signals of acceptance, that's something you can build on.

My meeting with Michelle went well, but it wasn't a slam dunk. She had some questions that I didn't have answers for. It's easy to sell to existing customers. It's a whole different ball game to bring in new customers. Michelle looked at me and asked, "How can Yes To bring incremental business? What's your plan there?"

My answer was simple: "I'll get back to you!"

Refining the Philosophy: The Four Love Points

Ido: We realized that Yes To had the ability to create an emotional connection with the consumer, but we wanted to know more about that connection. What was it, really? If we could get inside our female friends' heads, what would they really be thinking and feeling?

I was basically playing human Ping-Pong across the Atlantic at this point. And a big part of those flights was spent staring out of the window, thinking about our consumer, wondering who she was and how I could get her to care about what we were doing. I wanted to refine Yes To's magic "it" into a philosophy.

Michelle's concerns made sense; Walgreens had plenty of customers buying their conventional products already, so what were we going to do to bring a new customer inside? I told Lance what a great meeting we'd had and he went off to do one of those things he does best: create a financial model.

Meanwhile, I locked myself in my office and thought about Michelle's question. It seemed to boil down to one thing: How was I going to get women to care about this product and, more to the point, feel like the product cared about them?

What did this mysterious customer want? What was she thinking and feeling? Remember, this was 2006. The United States was about to hit a horrible recession, and the whole country was suffering under a very fractious and unpleasant cultural and political climate. It was a "no" moment, but here we were with a product that was all about "yes"! We wanted our brand to be relentlessly optimistic while many of our competitors focused on telling women no.

"No," as in:

- "No, you are not good enough, you need to get rid of those wrinkles."
- "No, you will not be loved if your skin isn't perfect."
- "No, your favorite products are bad for the environment and you are bad for using them!"

Screw "no." I thought about the loving, smart, funny, and all-around wonderful women in my life who had somehow been tricked into feeling bad about themselves because they had a few age spots or wrinkles, or because they'd put on a few pounds. I realized that the one thing our brand could do was to reverse this way of thinking. Instead of "No, I'm not good enough," I wanted our consumer to say, "Hell, yes! I'm just fine the way I am!"

Yes is a powerful word. It's enthusiasm, optimism, hope, and passion. We say yes to ideas or people that fill us with positive emotions and those positive emotions boil down to love. Something clicked in my head. I grabbed a Post-it note and wrote out our "Four Love Points":

- Will she love how the product works?
- Will she love how the product looks?
- Will she love the price?
- Will she love to tell her friends about it?

I realized that this idea of love and optimism was the magic "it" that Michelle was looking for. We put together a presentation, and a few weeks later I flew back to Illinois to present Michelle with our strategy for engaging with and appealing to a whole new set of customers.

I realized that the philosophy of Yes To had to be simple. Our customers value our honesty and simplicity. They don't want "Yes To Aleutian Sea Kelp" or "Yes To a Random Amazonian Berry Picked by Virgins." So we weren't going to waste our time creating those kinds of exotic products. Instead, we wanted our lines to feel like something everyone could be part of. We all feel comfortable with veggies: They aren't intimidating, and they're sitting in our fridges right this minute.

A brand guru once told us, "Your logo is way too big! Make it half the size and more subtle." I turned around and told him that our big, bright logo was the whole point. "Yes!" is the whole point. We didn't want to be the brand that stood up on a pedestal and told people how to live their lives. We just wanted to give our consumers great skin care and a pat on the back. We wanted to respect the fact that they were putting their hard-earned cash down on the counter for us and let them know that we would never compromise the quality of our product. That's it.

We had very little experience in creating a new brand, but we were able to look at everything we wanted the brand to stand for from day one, and that's what gave us the competitive advantage. Everything we did really had the opportunity to be straight from the heart, and love is such a big part of it. They're not called the "Four Like Points." We took every comment that we ever got from our customers to heart.

When we get a negative comment, it's like someone giving our child a bad report card. As a result, we are very motivated to make sure that everything we do has love in it.

If a brand can achieve those goals, no matter what the industry, then it's halfway there. If you were in a heavy industry, say cars or aviation, you'd want your customer to love your reliability and your safety. In the beauty industry it's often the little things, like when you open up your towelette package and it says, "wipe that smile *on* your face," that create the love between a consumer and a brand. And that's what we love about the beauty industry: We can make people feel better about themselves.

So that special connection that Yes To creates is all about love. It's not enough that our customers like our products; they need to feel that love is a two-way street. We genuinely feel love for our customers and our products. We want Yes To to give our customers reasons to love themselves, rather than finding things to dislike about their appearance. We don't believe in antiaging, we believe in age-refreshing; our customers shouldn't have to feel "anti" about anything! What a horrible thought. Why would any woman want a face cream that explicitly says she needs to fight nature and herself? Why not give her a product that adds positivity, rather than enforces negativity? It is all about feeling good about yourself. It's about refreshing yourself rather than controlling or "fixing" yourself. We love that we get to make a difference in people's lives and encourage them to smile rather than feel fear or resentment about themselves.

Michelle loved our plan to create a relationship with our customers. She also appreciated that I'd flown out from Tel Aviv to present it to her. But she had another question: "How are you going to fulfill my order — assuming I make one, that is?"

Good question. One of the pitfalls of moving fast is that sometimes your wheels are turning faster than your car can actually move. In this case, we had a great product and no way to produce the quantity Walgreens would need. So, back to Tel Aviv, more Skype sessions with Lance, a few tense negotiations with Uri, and I had an answer. We could do it. It meant that the factory would be working twenty-four hours a day, but it could happen.

I flew back to Chicago for a third time, popped into Michelle's office, and said, "It's all good. We can up production and we have a distribution center in the U.S. to ship to you." And that was that. A few days later, when I was home in Israel, I received an order for eight hundred units of each product for a trial on Walgreens.com.

We were beyond ecstatic. This was it: Yes To had hit the big time, and after all our sweating about production, the numbers were actually very doable. Our factory might have to go into overtime, but it would be able to turn out the product in time to ship. Great!

Surprise, once again, it wasn't a slam dunk. There was a catch; the trial would be online only. We would need to promote the hell out of Yes To and achieve a sell-through that impressed Michelle enough to prove that we could graduate from one point of sale (Walgreens.com) to the physical stores. This was our audition for the big time, and we could not screw it up.

But no sweat. We knew that once America had a taste of Yes To, we could meet those goals (whatever they were). We had faith.

Setting Up Shop

At the same time we were working our magic with Walgreens, we were also establishing some roots in Tel Aviv. Very quickly we realized that we needed some kind of headquarters that reflected who we were and what we were all about.

Ido: I'm a very visual person. I need my surroundings to be, at the very least, aesthetically pleasing, and ideally physically beautiful. If I can't have luxury, then I'll settle for interesting, and in our early days our offices reflected this.

When we decided to make the commitment to Yes To and prioritize it over all our other opportunities, we decided we needed an office in Israel. Real estate in Israel is just as expensive as it is in New York or San Francisco. We quickly realized that for our modest budget, we could have either a depressing and conventional space or something a bit odd but, hopefully, a bit more inspiring. We found a funky loft in an old converted mechanics workshop in an about-to-be-hip industrial neighborhood in Tel Aviv. Our street went: auto shop, brake shop, homeless guy, transmission shop, Yes To, falafel stand. In other words, the last thing you thought of when you drove up to our office was "beauty brand," but somehow the impact and surprise made you think, "Wow!"

Now that we had pretty much blown our budget on office space, we needed to think creatively in order to buy furniture. We had *Elle Decor* aspirations but a Nickel Shopper budget. After careful number-crunching, we decided we could budget for 50 percent IKEA, 40 percent flea market, and 10 percent fortuitous finds on the street. Funnily enough, this ratio ended up working well, and the mix of expected, unusual, and flat-out weird reflected us and our brand pretty well.

We had beautiful natural light, very high ceilings, and no walls. Instead, our boardroom was a space in the middle of the room enclosed by a huge print of a barcode. (I have to admit, today our conference rooms have walls, which even I concede are needed.) We commissioned a conference table from an industrial manufacturer that cost us about 25 percent what a traditional table would have cost. The morning I drove up to our office, parked, got out, and unlocked the door for the first time was phenomenal. We decided that from here on out, every office space we had needed to be special. Once again, it was a question of brand. Our space needed to serve double duty: It was our operational headquarters *and* a statement about who we were and what we were about.

Our office quickly became a kind of start-up hub. We were start-up entrepreneurs, our friends were start-up entrepreneurs, and so were all their friends. The most important thing that any entrepreneur needs—beyond one decent idea—is good friends and a supportive family. I was very fortunate to be surrounded by incredible mates who gave me the leeway I needed to be the crazy beauty entrepreneur by day and the adolescent they grew up with by night.

Being an entrepreneur can be the loneliest, most isolating job in the world. So get very good, very quickly, at finding people who understand what you are going through and who can act as a support system.

Being an entrepreneur in a start-up nation like Israel is an even more extreme experience, in both positive and negative ways. It's a situation fraught with opportunity. People are excited and willing to discuss new concepts. The problem is, they've seen hundreds of them—and three so far today. Everyone has something new. You have to sell your dream remembering that ultimately everyone in a start-up economy is trying to sell their dream, even the people you're pitching your dream to! So it's really important to see the real person, not the façade that person wants you to see.

We quickly found that we had incredible access to high-powered people: Because everyone in Israel wants to make connections and pitch their dreams, there are tons of networking events. And, unlike their equivalents in the United States or Australia, you can often meet the government officials you need to know over a cocktail and canapé. The smart businessperson focuses less on Facebook and more on creating a personal social network in the old-fashioned sense of the word. Take advantage of the fact that you are all in this together.

The other thing you learn in a start-up-nation, Israel in particular, is to try anything. If laughing and friendly cajoling don't work, try screaming, and if screaming doesn't work, try tears. When we first started Yes To, I had to beg someone to do something for me at least once a day. For the first two years of Yes To we treated every day like it might be our last. We thought of Yes To as a very, very fragile goose laying golden eggs.

You think I'm exaggerating?

The First Big Screw-up

Three weeks before the Walgreens order was due to ship, I was sitting in a great little coffee shop called Café Andre in Jaffa, sipping an espresso and feeling pretty good about my long-term prospects. My Nokia beeped and I saw a new e-mail about the order from the United States. I never really liked my Nokia; in fact, trying to run a business off of it made me crazy. You had to keep pressing a button to scroll down an e-mail, and if you opened a spreadsheet, I found it incredibly hard to read. I looked at this tiny phone, with its mishmashed numbers, and as I scanned the spreadsheet my stomach started to do a little dance. Something looked not quite right. The order numbers were off. What the hell?

I stepped out of the café and called our contractor in the United States.

"You made a mistake," I said. "The order was for eight hundred units of each product. You typed eight hundred cases. Can you fix it, please?"

The voice on the other end was quiet for a few seconds.

"Ido, I'm looking at the order. It's pretty clear. We need to ship eight hundred cases of each product unit tomorrow." I replied, "What are you talking about? You said we needed to send eight hundred of each item. I assumed you meant units; no one ever mentioned cases!"

I've had some bad moments in my life. The moment my parents told me we were broke. The moment my first girlfriend broke up with me. The moment when I realized that my hair was never coming back. This topped all of those, combined.

I was so shocked and horrified that I felt like laughing. A case contains twelve units of a product. So instead of manufacturing eight hundred units of each product, we needed to make ninety-six hundred. After three round-trips to Chicago, and the hardest work of my life building a great relationship with a critical account, it was all going to fall apart because of a misunderstanding over some pretty simple numbers.

The second-worst moment of that day was calling up the suppliers to our factory and explaining that we needed twelve times as much product as we had actually ordered, preferably tomorrow.

For about three hours I felt everything falling apart around me. I was stunned. I couldn't believe it. I couldn't see any way to fix this mess. After the initial freak-out subsided, I took a deep breath, jumped in my car, and spent the next twelve hours giving my inspirational speech to anybody who could possibly be persuaded to help. Factory managers, tube suppliers, printers, El Al booking agents, the guy standing in front of me in the line for coffee: They all heard the stirring story of an upstart young brand and the schmucks who'd risked everything to make it happen.

I called every factory in Israel that might be interested and willing to rush an order of Yes To Carrots out. Then I picked up the phone and dialed every shipping agent I knew. Twenty-four hours later I had a plan: We'd pay a premium to a few key factories to make the packaging of the product. Then, since a cargo boat would be too slow, we'd convinced El Al to lease us two of their 767s for two "carrots only" flights across the Atlantic. Do you know how much it costs to lease two airliners for twenty-four hours? Let's just say it's painfully, horrifyingly expensive. We'd take a guaranteed loss—even if every unit sold—but we would fulfill our order and keep our promise to our new partner.

Lance: Against all the odds we got the product manufactured, shipped, and received. Now we just had to sell it. Our order with Walgreens was an online trial. If we wanted to become a permanent account, we had to prove that we were a viable product that could connect with customers in a meaningful way.

Remember, this was a couple of generations ago in online retail. By December 2006, Walgreens.com was still a very new concept for the company. They were trying to play catch-up in the e-commerce game, but in truth none of the major drug retailers had quite yet cracked the online world. Our task was even harder. We had to outsell our competitors online and bring new customers to Walgreens.com to prove that we were worthy of a real-world, bricks-and-mortar rollout. The initial order to fulfill the online trial was already bigger than we'd ever expected, so we knew we had a Herculean task to move that stock and win a place in the golden aisles of the world's largest drugstore chain. We knew the stakes were high, and we were ready to throw everything we had at it.

Lance: We had quickly run through the money that the Investor had given us, and we were down to our last $100,000. The majority of the funds had gone into rushing the last-minute order and air-freighting it to Walgreens so that we didn't completely screw up our first big opportunity. Even though Walgreens owed us for the stock we had sold them, we knew that we wouldn't be seeing this cash until well after the online trial had ended. So we had to come up with a marketing effort that was targeted, unique, and affordable. We looked at placing a print advertisement in a leading magazine, but with only $100,000, this was way out of our price range. So we settled on online marketing and found an Israeli firm that had experience in this field and did a hell of a job making us believe they were capable of helping us bring home the Walgreens trophy.

Ido: We were bleeding money on the paid online marketing ads. The point was to get online customers to purchase Yes To products from Walgreens.com, but our instinct was that they weren't doing much. We didn't know for sure because Walgreens was not able to tell us, mid-trial, if we were meeting their expectations. I felt like one of the most pivotal opportunities of our lives was slipping through our fingers. It was Hail Mary time again. We needed to do something that was game-changing. We were not going down without a fight.

Lance: Three weeks into the eight-week trial we finally got some feedback on numbers and it wasn't great. I knew that if we carried on that way we weren't going to impress the buyer enough to get into physical stores. I looked at Ido and told him: "You'd better come up with something big, and quickly. If we don't make this work, our cash flow will be a disaster and we will be in a whole world of pain!"

Ido stared at me.

"Don't worry, Lance, I've got a plan!"

Uh-oh.

"We're going to do an ad in *Cosmopolitan!*"

"That's crazy, Ido! Do you know how expensive that is? And you have to book weeks in advance."

"Sure, it's crazy," he replied, "but it might just be crazy enough to work!"

Ido: I knew that with only a few weeks of the online trial left to run, putting an ad in a leading beauty magazine would not have a major effect on sales, but I actually had another plan in my head. I had consistently told Walgreens that we would support a national rollout with a comprehensive print and in-store marketing program. So if we weren't going to blow her away with sales numbers during the online trial, we were going to blow them away with delivering on the marketing promises. I made a quick call to an agency friend of ours in Los Angeles who helped us pick up a last-minute advertisement in the next issue of *Cosmopolitan.* It was going to cost us $75,000 — and that was the heavily discounted, last-minute rate — but I knew that it would just coincide with the last two weeks of the trial and hopefully give it enough boost to get us over the finish line in time. Most important, I told him to start preparing the copy and artwork, and in the most conspicuous font and position, boldly write: AVAILABLE EX-CLUSIVELY AT WALGREENS.COM.

Placing your brand in a national magazine is a big thing in the beauty world and especially for retailers. The bigger players who have national coverage and vast distribution through multiple retailers focus on this kind of marketing. They can earn a significant return on their investment from such an expensive form of outreach. For a tiny upstart like Yes To to take out an ad in *Cosmopolitan* was a brave and very loud statement. To take out an ad when we had distribution in only *one* channel meant we were worthy of being institutionalized.

But hopefully this crazy move would impress Walgreens just enough to think that we were, well, crazy enough to do the same thing on a bigger scale should we gain access to their physical stores.

As it turns out, the ad in *Cosmopolitan* came out just in time, and the effect it had on sales completely blew us away! By this I mean that we were stunned to find out that it hadn't done anything. I'd be amazed if the ad sold one bottle of moisturizer. (This was a lesson we were going to learn twice, as you will see later on.)

Lance: We were now down to practically no cash flow, and while I contemplated which blunt instrument I was going to hit Ido over the head with, he traveled to Chicago to meet with Michelle and her team. Ido had done everything he could to make sure that everyone who mattered at Walgreens had seen that *Cosmo* ad and was well aware that we had given Walgreens.com a very prominent mention in our advertisement.

Meanwhile, I was in Sydney, trying to sleep, knowing that on the other side of the world my partner was about to hear the results that would make or break our business. I tossed and turned fitfully and waited for the red light on my BlackBerry to blink. Loren was fast asleep next to me, and all I could think about was how I was going to take care of her and the kids if this deal didn't go through. What would I do if we had to tank the whole Yes To business before it even really got started? All I was hoping for was that the Walgreens team would give us another chance to show them that we could sell in a trial across a few hundred physical stores. That way we could have another shot at it and I could keep the company's cash flow alive long enough to pull another rabbit out of the hat.

At three in the morning, Sydney time, the phone rang. I jumped up, well aware that this was going to be one of the most pivotal moments of my life.

"Ido! Is that you?"

"No, Lance, it's your fairy godmother. Who else would call you at three in the morning?"

"Cut the bull, mate, what happened? I'm dying here!"

"Well, I have some good news and some bad news. Which do you want to hear first?"

"Just give me the good news. I can't handle any bad news right now."

"The good news is that they were really happy with the online trial results. Walgreens.com is still pretty new for them and apparently our sales results were very good compared to our competitors'. They want all sixteen Yes To products and they want to distribute them in all 5,800 stores!"

"[Censored.] Are you kidding me? That's the best news I've ever heard!"

By now my whole family was wide awake and wondering what the hell was going on. The kids were crying because they thought their dad had gone crazy.

"What could possibly be the bad news, Ido?"

"Well, they want all the products in the U.S.A. in three months' time. Otherwise, they won't take the order."

Not even this major logistical challenge could dampen my excitement. It was the most exhilarating conversation of my life. I couldn't believe that we were going from selling in ten stores in Israel and one online site to selling in 5,800 stores with the world's biggest drugstore retailer. It was the biggest breakthrough of our careers, and I was so happy to be sharing it with Ido on the phone, my wife next to me, and my kids in their rooms next door.

Ido: As I walked out of the Walgreens meeting, I was jumping up and down for joy on the inside, while staying very calm on the outside. I remember walking to my car in the freezing parking lot, getting in, and thinking to myself, "Alright, that's incredible, wow, amazing, we did it, our lives are forever changed. Now, how the hell are we going to do this?"

From that moment on, Lance and I didn't even have time to celebrate the success. (Which I now regret. Lance, I think next time we are in the same time zone we should buy a bottle of Blue Label and drink the whole thing in one sitting!)

The *Cosmopolitan* ad strategy had worked. They were intrigued about what we would do next to move product off the shelves in their stores. If we were going to be so bold with them, they were going to take a chance on us as well.

But we had a huge challenge ahead of us. Not only did we have to produce and ship the goods in record time to arrive in the United States within three months, but we had to find the money to pay for all of this! The initial order was for three million dollars' worth of product. Here we were, less than three months old as a company, and we had an order from one of the world's biggest retailers for three million dollars. We still have a copy of the check framed and hanging on the wall in our office today.

Why Did We Present to Walgreens First?

Against all the odds (many of them self-created) our online Walgreens trial had been a success. Walgreens' customers had been sufficiently interested to try this innovative, natural brand. We'd fulfilled Walgreens' requirement to bring a new kind of customer to their website and sales were good. The Walgreens team had seen — many times — that we were willing to do anything to make this work, and the end result was that they had faith in us. They were willing to take it to the next level, with one big "but." Walgreens required that we give them a one-year exclusive *and* a universal rollout. That meant that all 5,800 stores had to have the same products on their shelves at the same time.

Remember, at this time, other than our online deal with Walgreens.com, our entire distribution amounted to about ten stores in Israel. And we had just promised a nationwide rollout in the United States within *ninety* days.

Your first big customer is a big deal. Your first big *exclusive* customer is a really big deal.

Going exclusive with Walgreens was a risky move. We knew we would get only one shot with brick-and-mortar U.S. retailers; we had to tread carefully and avoid offending or angering another retailer by going exclusive right out of the gate. Retailers can get frustrated if they can't get your product when they want it.

Our decision to go exclusive with Walgreens boiled down to a few key factors. Walgreens was the first national chain drugstore to embrace naturals and invest in them, and we had a great connection and relationship with Walgreens already. More important, Walgreens had beauty advisors in most of their stores, dedicated staff who advised and educated customers in the beauty section. We would be able to offer them incentives to focus on Yes To and explain our brand to the consumer. The beauty advisors were like an ace up our sleeve, and they were incentivized for every sale they made.

We may be huge fans of big and fast, but we also believe in good. We went exclusive with Walgreens because their needs perfectly aligned with the product we were developing. Going exclusive can be risky and it is not an easy decision. Exclusivity made sense for us because building one rock-solid partnership with a large retailer seemed to offer us the best chance of success. But each business needs to look at the pros and cons to determine what works best for them. Before you make a decision either way, consider these factors:

Our Top Reasons to Go Exclusive

1. Exclusivity gives you a chance to build a true partnership in which each relies on the other's success.
2. It allows you to develop a long-term sense of loyalty with your retail partner that can see you through hard times.
3. You'll get a lot more "goodies" — special treatment — with an exclusive relationship.
4. Exclusivity gives you time to focus on one customer, refining and perfecting how your company does things.
5. You can create pent-up demand in the marketplace. As soon as our exclusivity ended we were in discussions with Target and Duane Reade, and they were eager and excited to go into business with us.

Our Top Reasons Not to Go Exclusive

1. Going exclusive minimizes your exposure in the market and can increase your risk.
2. You are putting all of your eggs in one basket. If you fail, the odds of another retailer stocking you are minimal.
3. You're not getting a meaningful return on investment on your marketing effort unless it's specifically in-store marketing.
4. It sets a potentially problematic precedent. Other outlets, such

as grocery stores, will also want exclusives. You have the potential to alienate your exclusive retailer's competitors and other channels.

In February 2007 we had a handshake deal with Walgreens to do an exclusive rollout in their stores. Our exclusive with Walgreens meant that we didn't need to do a lot of industry interaction within the United States. However, we could go out and meet international buyers, and so that's just what we did. We attended an international trade event in Monaco where we met key people from the international retail world. This was our debut on the global market, and we went all out to make an impact.

Sometimes there has to be a certain element of smoke and mirrors in business. Not in the quality of your product or in the accuracy of your accounting, but in the way you present yourself to the world. In our business, a big part of this presentation is attending the annual industry conferences. Magazines and advertising are for the consumer, but these events are for buyers, and they are equally important, if not more so. A lot of brands launch modestly, but as you know by now, that is not how we do things. We were determined that when we made our formal debut as an in-store brand, it would be a tap-dancing, barn-raising, full-on production.

At the Monaco event, most brands get a hotel room and set up a desk; we turned our entire hotel room into a Yes To Carrots zone. Everything was branded. It was a complete Yes To immersion experience, from the carrot-juice bar to the large, branded bags that everyone received when they walked out of the room (showing them off to other retailers in the hallways).

We executed everything perfectly. It went great. Meanwhile, our exclusive deal with Walgreens meant that we couldn't go after business with other U.S. retailers. We honored the word and the spirit of this agreement and purposefully avoided talking with other U.S. chain brands.

At the very end of the show, just as we were packing up, the two most senior people at one of Walgreens' biggest competitors walked in and tried to convince us to go into their stores rather than Walgreens. We told them that we had a handshake deal with Walgreens and that we were going to stand by this commitment, and that we couldn't walk away from it. Although they were unhappy with our answer, I think they respected our loyalty and our commitment to standing by our deal.

The interesting aspect of this story is that the retailer we talked to decided that if they couldn't have us, they'd find another brand just like us and make that one *their* exclusive natural brand. They chose a great little brand, with nice branding and effective products, but it didn't work, and they dropped them a few years later.

The number one mistake this "Not Yes To" brand made was refusing to do any price promotion or discounting in the retailer's catalogs, so there was no incentive for a potential new customer to try it. If you're going to launch a brand, the first thing you need to offer your potential customers is a trial. This is even more important if you're going exclusive, because you've automatically reduced the number of potential customers out there. Exclusive sounds important, but it also intensifies the process of introducing your brand. If you mess it up, you might not get a second chance.

The second-biggest mistake the "Not Yes To" brand made was that they seemed to mimic our advertising strategy, which, frankly, wasn't working that well for *us*. It did an even worse job for them. Finally, they vastly over-promised what they could deliver. We heard rumors on the industry grapevine that "Not Yes To" had promised they would be featured on *Oprah* and that they would get other meaningful press through their existing connections. Neither of these things happened, and their failure to achieve what they had promised undermined the brand in the eyes of their retailer.

This leads into an important point: You can have the best product in the world, one that you know your customer will love, but if you can't get that customer to try your product, you're sunk. Your retailers are your partners, but you can't expect them to do the heavy lifting of selling your product once it's on their shelves; that is your job.

As you'll see, we didn't really understand just how challenging it would be to reach potential customers when we launched in brick-and-mortar stores in the United States. On some level, we figured that just being there, on the shelves, would be enough. This was a huge misunderstanding on our part and one that would almost sink our company in the very near future.

Advertising and Marketing

Our experiences with conventional advertising have been mixed, to say the least. As you'll see, one ill-planned ad campaign almost torpedoed our company. Currently we don't run advertising in the traditional sense; you generally won't see ads for our products in a magazine or on a billboard in the United States. We are open to revisiting this strategy, but for now we have no compelling reason to change. It's important to put aside your pride and vanity and *not* automatically commission an ad campaign just because it seems like the right thing to do.

So, here's the story of Yes To's ever-evolving advertising strategy, a section we like to call:

How to Get Ahead (with a Few Big Muck-ups and
One Good Decision) in Advertising

Right after Walgreens committed to our online trial, we blew a huge percentage of our remaining capital on the one-off print ad at the back of *Cosmopolitan.* It was messy, off-message, confusing to the reader, and did almost nothing to generate sales for our brand. It *did* show how committed we were to making this trial work, and that was useful for our overall relationship with Walgreens, but that was about all.

So, when the dust had settled and we could breathe again, we were understandably gun-shy about moving ahead with another advertising campaign. At the same time, after our successful online trial we now had an eighteen-month exclusive deal with Walgreens to sell Yes To in stores. We *had* to do something to make sure that sales were phenomenal during this period.

At this time, Walgreens had around six thousand outlets in the United States and was opening a new store every eight hours. We had originally started our business in Israel, where the largest retail chain has a hundred twenty stores. In other words, we were absolutely flabbergasted and gob-smacked at the size of what we were dealing with.

Suddenly, we needed to shift some serious amounts of product. We felt a mix of excitement and fear. Excitement because, on one level, we had finally cracked it. We had an invitation to sell our products on the world's biggest stage with one of the greatest retailers in the world. Fear because we read the writing in the fine print of the purchase order:

SALE OR RETURN

WARNING: Hold off on the Ferrari. Getting *into* a major national retailer does not mean you have made it big-time just yet!

Most people in our industry try for their whole career to break into a major retailer with a product. When they finally do, they break out that bottle of Blue Label whiskey, buy their partner a Tiffany tennis bracelet or Rolex, and throw a celebration like they just got accepted into Harvard. But getting listed — the industry term for getting accepted onto the shelves of a retailer — at a major retailer is just the first baby step in a sales journey akin to a marathon.

Retail buyers are smart and experienced. With the risks they are taking by paying you millions for your product to be on their shelves, they know they need some protection. This usually comes in the form of three little words: SALE OR RETURN. What this means is that when you launch with a retailer, you generally have a twelve-month window to make it work, and if it doesn't work the retailer can send your unsold stock back for a full refund. So, for us, as big as the in-store exclusive was, it could also potentially ruin us if it didn't work. If we didn't make meaningful sales, and quickly, we were gone. We literally couldn't afford to fail.

Despite our previous experience with our one-off *Cosmo* ad, we decided to give print advertising another shot. We needed to reach large numbers of women, and reach them quickly.

This was one of the bad decisions in our story.

We realized that we needed help, so we took a few meetings and signed up with an L.A.-based ad shop. They put together an ad that, in retrospect, was all wrong: not spectacularly bad, just irrelevant in both design and copy. The ad tried to do too much; it tried to tell the whole story and showcase the entire line of products rather than focusing on a specific product or category. Bottom line, it looked good, but it didn't have a strong call-to-action element for consumers to go out and buy the products. What we should have done was test the ad in a local area, see the results, and change our approach accordingly.

The biggest mistake we made was not the ineffective ad, it was assuming that because we were in six thousand stores, we were available for purchase "everywhere." This couldn't have been further from the truth. (Question: How many Walgreens do you see in Manhattan? Answer: Not many.) As a result, many potential customers in key areas could not find us on the shelves of other stores after seeing our ads.

All of a sudden we were placing four big bets at once:

1. Sales will materialize.
2. We are advertising in the right places.
3. We will get a return on investment on our advertising dollar.
4. The strategy would work because we'd been taught in business school that it would.

We were so wrapped up in the brand that we made the huge rookie mistake of not stepping outside of our situation and reassessing what we were doing. It is vitally important to look at what you are doing from an outsider's perspective and ask yourself, "How is this actually going to work?"

We had very little spare capital. We had a very small customer base. If we'd stopped to listen to our guts, we might have considered that our company had succeeded when we did things *differently*. Yet here we were, committing every spare dollar to the most traditional marketing strategy in the book. Even more important, we were focusing on the very last step — a traditional ad campaign — when we should have been focusing on the basics. We had things all backwards. It was like we were playing our closing pitcher in the first innings. (Go, Giants!)

As it turned out, we had put all of our eggs in a very fragile basket.

The print campaign was designed to drive major sales, and we believed it would. After all, we'd hired an ad agency and a PR agency and we'd launched a national campaign. How could it not work? But for all the time and effort and money — and all the exposure in the major magazines — our campaign did almost nothing for our sales.

Why? In retrospect it was a combination of several things. For one, the brand was too new, and potential customers didn't know where to find us in the store even if they were aware of Yes To. Remember, at this point natural beauty was a new category for Walgreens and it was not something their existing customers were necessarily looking for. For another, the ad wasn't great and the placement was terrible. We were buying remnant space in a wide variety of magazines at the last minute, which meant that we might have a prime spot at the front of the magazine or be stuck in the back. There was no consistency in how we presented ourselves to our customers.

Side lesson of this story: This was primarily Ido's decision.

Ido: I had to convince Lance, and he ended up supporting me in it, but it was a terrible decision. Lance pointed out that if it didn't work, we'd "be out of money in six months." But it was my area of expertise and my call. It was my wrong call, but we supported each other through this. Once we realized that the ad campaign was a massive waste of resources and a total distraction for both of us, we reevaluated. We had $80,000 left in the bank. That was literally all we had. My gut feeling was that we had to do something big with this remaining money, and that it was better to blow everything on one last shot of making an impact, rather than let it slowly melt away as our company died in front of us.

"The way we are going to salvage it is to do an online competition," I said. Note that this was *still* my call, even though I had screwed up my last call. I was the marketing guy, and Lance, to his eternal credit, still respected this. He understood that a great sales and marketing guy could screw up and still be a great sales and marketing guy. So he gave me his blessing and we launched the MySpace "Face of Yes To" campaign.

We used our last dollars to rent and decorate a van and sent it to various college campuses around the United States. We knew we had a brilliant product that people would love if they only gave it a try. Our pitch was that we were looking for a man and a woman to be the faces of the brand. We offered a ten-thousand-dollar cash prize, an editorial in *Elle*, and a year's supply of Yes To products. College kids love free stuff and they loved our campaign: It was unusual, fun, and funny. We hired a bunch of young, outgoing people to man the truck, and we gave potential customers a chance to try the product. We knew we had a brilliant product that people would love if they gave it a try.

College students started talking via social media about how much they loved Yes To. We ended up with over a hundred thirty thousand people voting in the final contest, and everyone who voted was given coupons and information about our products. It also let us collate hundreds of thousands of e-mail addresses of people who were interested in our products and start to have a conversation with customers who were already interested in who we were and what we were doing. (Remember, this was during the infancy of sites like Facebook, so those numbers were very impressive at the time.) It drove a huge amount of traffic to Walgreens. Unlike our ad campaign, the online campaign *did* help generate business. The competition was the draw to get people engaged, but the incredible products were what kept people around.

Lance: I think the big takeaway from our experience with that national ad campaign is this: Don't try to do it all at once. Yes, when you are a struggling start-up, you need to make big decisions, but be smart about it. DON'T DO A SUPERBOWL AD. Do it as moderately as you can while still making an impact and being creative.

The "Face of Yes To" contest finally got that needle moving. Brand awareness was up, and even more important, Walgreens saw that we were willing to do anything and go the extra mile to make our deal with them work. They appreciated that, and that good feeling was just as valuable as the bump in sales.

The second big takeaway is actually the biggest secret in the success of Yes To: Just do what works. The thing that works for us is to talk directly with our customers. We've learned that in-store execution is really important. You need to make sure that your shelf looks great and is always fully stocked. In-store programs, such as catalogs, or beauty salespeople who can answer customer questions immediately, are more valuable than ad space. Doing in-store offers is a great way for us to have that ongoing communication with our customers, and it's beneficial to our retailer since it's a Walgreens customer walking into a Walgreens store looking to shop. Eventually, we realized that the single best advertising for us is the retail circular program. A tiny picture in a Walgreens, Duane Reade, or Target catalog can increase sales 200 percent a week. As a result, we don't do print in the United States; the dollars we spend on in-store activity are a much better return on investment for us.

You will never be able to outspend the big guys (for us that's Procter & Gamble and L'Oreal) in traditional marketing spends such as print and television. We will always be dwarfed by the multinationals. Your best chance of beating the big guys is at the store level. Try to entice the customers that they push into the stores with their big spends. Try and swing the purchase decision at the last moment so customers buy your brand instead of theirs. Of course, you'll need to do some kind of brand awareness, but let the big guys do the hard work of presenting new and innovative products to customers, and then use on-shelf tactics, pricing, and packaging to steal the sale at the last minute.

We learned these lessons the hard way, and we learned that this is the deep, dark secret for the big boys. Advertising is less important than things like catalogs, endcaps, and getting secondary placement, that is, being placed in another part of the store in addition to your primary shelf space. For us this might mean placement both in the beauty aisle and in the trial or travel aisle. You do pay an indirect cost because usually you do some kind of offer associated with the secondary placement. The retailer wants you to advertise, but they make money if you support their circular program because it drives people specifically to their store. A Yes To ad drives people to all sorts of stores, but a catalog drives people specifically to *their* store.

Partnering with our retailers and working with them for our mutual benefit is one of the core pillars of how we do business. The second pillar for us is PR; we have a fantastic PR agency and we believe firmly that the first agency expense for any new business should be PR. A great PR agency can give you a fantastic return on investment that is significantly more than anything other than in-store marketing.

Let's assume you have a really incredible brand, product, service, or invention, but a modest budget that won't stretch far enough for a meaningful ad buy. There are many options for how to spend your hard-earned dough. For us, however, the most effective and efficient use of time and funds has been public relations. From day one, PR has been the number one driver of our marketing plan. We had a very small budget in year one, but we managed to get over 250 million domestic impressions in magazines, newspapers, and on TV. We even made it onto *The Price Is Right*.

Ido: Today in the United States we get over one billion impressions annually. In 2012, a video interview I appeared in won an Emmy Award. It's quite remarkable what you can achieve if you put yourself out there.

PR, PR, PR!

1. Choose the right size PR agency. This is money well spent! Over the years we have worked with both small and large PR agencies. I recommend a smaller agency if you are new or have a limited budget. A smaller agency will give you a lot more attention; the senior team rather than an intern will do the work!

2. Choose a PR agency focused in your industry. I recently saw a restaurant that was being represented by a tech PR firm.

Wrong, all wrong! A PR firm focused in your industry will have deep-rooted relationships with the right editors and producers and will get you more effective press. Make sure you call their references prior to signing and find out how effective the agency has been in getting press and results for their clients. Snoop around and ask questions.

3. When your PR company sets you up in a meeting with the press, always be consistent, honest, and authentic! Build a long-term relationship by being approachable and real. No one wants to write about a jerk.

4. Show up on a regular basis: Ido travels to New York four times a year to meet with beauty editors to share "what's new." Make sure you always have something new and exciting to talk about. Be "newsworthy." Do everything in your power to build a solid and real relationship with the relevant editors in your industry.

5. Be thankful! If you get a great piece written about you, make sure you thank the person who wrote it.

6. Be excited! No one wants to meet with a boring individual. If you aren't excited about what you're doing, how the heck do you expect the press to get excited about it?

We eventually reviewed all our advertising efforts and partnered promotions and realized that the single most effective way for us to reach our customer was through in-store circulars. They're not glamorous or sexy. There are no expensive photo shoots or supermodels involved. But they really, really work for us.

In addition, we've gotten huge benefits from giving our customers financial incentives to try new products, such as offering two-for-ones, or "freebates."

We were, as you've seen, willing to do anything to make our exclusive with Walgreens work. And this is the attitude you have to have in order to take full advantage of an opportunity like this. You always have to have something else up your sleeve in case your marketing and promotion efforts fall short. If you believe in your product and your product is truly good, and you want people to try it, then you have to give them some motivation to pick up a tube of whatever you are selling. In-store sampling is key. So is putting coupons on one product to drive people to try another one. If your "product" isn't actually a product, you need to figure out ways to get people to try your services, even if it means giving away a sample of your ideas or work for free. Look at how Internet companies offer "freemium" versions of their software; this allows potential customers to try software before they commit to purchasing it. Can you apply this idea to your business? Don't be afraid that if you share your ideas, people will steal them; the benefits of getting out there and wholeheartedly pitching yourself have bigger potential dividends than keeping information or ideas proprietary.

In February 2008 we decided to make another big push based on this idea of giving away products to lure potential new customers. One of the promises that I'd made to Walgreens when we first started working together was that Yes To would bring new customers into their stores. The "Face of" contest had partially succeeded, but we still needed to give our efforts one more kick in the pants to get things going. Walgreens loved us, but part of that love was being a pushy parent and encouraging us to try harder and grow faster. They had actually liked our print campaign, and more important, they respected the effort we were putting into making this relationship work. So they wanted to know, "What's your next big investment?"

We wanted to do something that would bring new faces into the stores and in front of our products. We needed something that every potential customer would respond to, which meant offering them the one thing that everyone loves: a full-size, free product. Barb, an amazing marketing expert and divisional merchandise manager at

Walgreens, gently nudged us to try a freebate. A freebate is just what it sounds like: A customer buys a tub of Yes To from Walgreens, fills out a form, mails it in, and eventually is fully reimbursed for the purchase price of the product. We were scared of this, initially; it seemed a great way to ruin our business. Barb reassured us that in her experience a freebate was the best way for a fledgling brand to accelerate the process of winning over new customers. As nervous as we were, we also believed wholeheartedly in Barb's wisdom and decided to go for it. Turns out she was right.

Freebates are, for obvious reasons, unbelievably expensive; however, they are a slightly deferred expense. It would take up to four months to refund our customers, and the payments were staggered depending on how quickly customers mailed in their coupons. This tiny time buffer would (hopefully) give us enough time to recoup the investment. Our goal was simple: We wanted as many people as possible to try, and love, our products.

The freebate was our way of putting our money where our mouth was. We truly believed that letting potential customers try our product was the greatest incentive to get them to buy it. And we decided to give them a chance to try our number one, most popular, life-changing product: Yes To Carrots body butter.

Funnily enough, after many marketing decisions where we overestimated the effect of a particular strategy or campaign, we actually underestimated the power of the freebate. We had budgeted for a hundred thousand sales of the body butter, total, but in just one month we sold a hundred fifty thousand! We actually sold more than one million dollars of product in the first week!

Yes, we had to reimburse the cost of the body butter (and eat the cost of the reimbursement). But we quickly realized that when customers picked up the body butter they were also grabbing other products to try at the same time (because the butter was "free"). Almost by accident we had a highly targeted and absolutely fantastic campaign that brought us new customers *and* got existing customers to try new items in our range.

From a mathematical perspective, it worked perfectly. Prior to this we had spent the equivalent of hundreds of dollars per customer on print campaigns designed to get women into stores and to create long-term customers. With the freebate we were spending $13.50 to acquire a new customer who might then buy a body butter every month. Although the initial outlay was expensive (if delayed), the return — a customer who loves the body butter and buys it consistently — was well worth it.

Lance: At this stage I was still somewhat on the periphery of the Yes To action in the United States. Up to this point I had never even seen our product on the shelf or met anyone at Walgreens in person. I was in Israel, dealing with manufacturing and people problems, while Ido was having a great time making magic happen in the States. My main job was still very much behind the scenes, splitting time between Yes To and Trendtrade (which was paying our bills!) and doing everything I could, short of scrounging for change in our couch cushions, to keep the cash flow in the black at Yes To.

I've known and loved Ido for many years, and one thing I know and love about him is his relentless positivity. You could tell him he needs to build *another* bridge over the River Kwai, by Monday, and he'd approach it with 100 percent enthusiasm and a resounding "No problem!" This is wonderful, but it also means that I've gotten used to filtering his enthusiasm through my own, more pragmatic lens. There are times when I'm the worrying Eeyore to his ever-cheerful Piglet, and the reality of any situation lies somewhere between our two perspectives.

So as Yes To's relationship with Walgreens developed, I got used to hearing these incredibly enthusiastic, impassioned "he said, then she said, then he said" accounts of Ido's meetings with Michelle and her team.

"It's unbelievable, Lance!" he'd say. "They love us. Things are going well. We've launched and the freebate is through the roof. People are clutching tubs of body butter to their chests and crying in the streets!"

I'll admit to having been a little skeptical. Ido's positive attitude about everything means that sometimes you think he's putting a good spin on something bad. After running what Ido was saying through my Excessively Enthusiastic Partner Filter, I heard something more along the lines of: "You probably don't need to sell your firstborn just yet."

When Ido came back from his fifth meeting with Walgreens, he said, "Lance, I'm not even going to tell you, it was so awesome."

"Come on, Ido. Tell me one bad thing about the meeting." When he couldn't come up with one negative, I decided that I needed to see what was happening for myself. I flew out to the next meeting to meet with Ido and Michelle, but when we walked into the conference room the whole Walgreens team was waiting for us. The main point of the meeting was to lay out the strategic vision of the brand for the next two to three years. Our online exclusive with Walgreens was almost up, and I figured we really needed to impress them and make sure they'd keep us on. I had everything short of a talking dog in my briefcase because I figured we were going to have to put on a pretty impressive show. But as the meeting went on I realized something interesting: They seemed to be trying to impress *us*. Even more interesting, they seemed to be giving us reasons to be continually committed to *them*.

I'll freely admit that I walked into that office convinced that Ido was overly optimistic about our long-term future at Walgreens. And yet, ten minutes in, they asked us, "How many new products are you developing?"

Ido stood up and gave the pitch of his life, outlining all our dreams and ideas for Yes To's near-term future in a two-year plan. At this point, we were really gung-ho on developing the Yes To Tomatoes and Yes To Cucumbers lines. We saw how focusing solely on carrots was too limiting and that we needed to appeal to customers with other skin types and skin-care needs. Kathy, the then director of beauty at Walgreens, who I now realized was going to be *my* new best friend, too, looked thoughtful for a second and said, "What if I give you another shelf?"

"Another shelf!" I exclaimed. This was nuts. Was she pranking us?

Another shelf is like the mayor of San Francisco being given the budget to build another Golden Gate Bridge and, oh, maybe another airport. Or your wife telling you, "Let's have an open relationship." Or getting to buy Park Place twice in Monopoly. It just doesn't happen. When someone offers you a shelf, you don't walk away from it. It's the Holy Grail.

Full credit to Ido, he didn't even blink. He just smiled and said, "That would be fantastic. We can expedite the production of Yes To Tomatoes and Yes To Cucumbers."

Then they upped the ante even further.

"We're thinking lip balms, in two fishbowls on every cash register of every store. Do you think you can do it?"

Now, Burt's Bees dominates the natural-lip-balm category, so this was a very aggressive move to beat them at their own business. Without hesitating we both looked at her and said: "Of course!"

As we walked out of the meeting, I turned to Ido and said, "Frank, you were right." Ido, being a somewhat cocky bastard, just laughed and said, "Told you so."

This was the single most exciting forty minutes of my career in business.

Of course, all business stories have their ups and downs. This was a huge meeting for us in terms of launching our Tomatoes and Cucumbers lines, but we actually messed up on the lip balms. Our lip balms were fantastic. We made a superior product that had a luxurious feel, a great smell, and worked really well. We had the best possible placement, too. But we messed up on the pricing. When we developed the balms we thought that people would pay a premium for organic, as opposed to natural, lip balm. We were three times as expensive as ChapStick and about 20 percent more expensive than Burt's Bees. What we should have done was lowered our margin and underpriced Burt's Bees.

The bigger-picture ramifications were that we found ourselves overextended in two ways. First, we'd overextended ourselves on the balms. The eventual order was for two million units, but ultimately we had to take a big return on them. To this day, if you have a meeting with me or Ido, you will walk away with armfuls of lip balms! We'd eat them for breakfast if we could. We'd also overextended ourselves in terms of operations. By this point, we were supplying Walgreens with twenty new products and still operating out of Israel only. Our U.S. workforce was one employee in Chicago! We realized that if we were going to continue to grow and create a sustainable business, we needed to bring on the right financial and strategic partners to help us, and that's when we decided to raise more capital.

7

The Investor Dating Game

I T WAS NEARING THE END of 2007, and we were ecstatic to have
achieved our second major milestone. The first major milestone was
getting listed at Walgreens. The second was surviving the stresses and
struggles of the listing! We had performed well. We'd created enough
excitement and evidence of sales to take Yes To from a concept brand
to a brand that consumers would repeatedly purchase. This was incredibly important. Repeat sales are what retailers look for in order to
establish whether your brand will make it or not.

Ido: By now, major retailers such as Target, Duane Reade, and
Sephora Europe had approached us, and we had initiated serious discussions with all of them. We were nearing the end of exclusivity with
Walgreens and we could feel the huge momentum building behind
us. It was that sweet spot in a company's life when your brand becomes so hot no retailer wants to lose the chance to list you. But every
time I called Lance to tell him about a new listing at a new retailer, his
response was quieter than the time before.

Lance: Ido was doing a sublime job of winning new retailers, but
it started to feel like the speed we were traveling at was way beyond

the safe driving limits of the Yes To vehicle. All I could think of was that the faster we went, the bigger the crash would be if we were to hit even a small stone along the way. We had already made a couple of severe screw-ups, but thanks to limited distribution at the time — being in only one retailer — we were able to pivot and realign without doing too much damage.

However, if we screwed up in multiple retailers in relatively small ways, such as inadequate product quality, slow delivery, or inferior customer service, it would be disastrous. At this stage we had only five full-time employees besides Ido and myself; only one was based in the United States, the rest were in Israel, on the other side of the world. I started to do the working capital calculations to see what the business would require if we brought on major retailers such as Target and Sephora, and I quickly realized that we were way undercapitalized. My experience at PwC and Trendtrade had shown me that there is just as much chance for a fast-growing company to fail due to being undercapitalized as there is for a company lacking sales. Fortunately, raising capital was one of my stronger points, and I had the world's greatest salesman as my partner to help me do it as quickly as possible.

Ido: Let's just say I am more used to pitching to carefree buyers and brand owners than to serious, suit-wearing investment bankers and private-equity guys. So Lance sat me down for a few lessons, in this case on corporate etiquette and formality. There might be the potential for orange socks and a bit of flair, but the European kiss on both cheeks and "I'll get back to you on that one" was not going to cut it with time-is-money bankers.

Lance: Even though we had the Investor, his background was primarily in real estate. We needed to raise upwards of $14 million to build the working capital to support the inventory needs and resource requirements of supplying multiple major retailers in the United States. I knew that this amount meant we needed to focus on a limited number of private-equity players in the United States who considered investing in consumer goods companies. One possibility was to get Ido to cold call most of these private-equity players, which may have yielded a positive response. However, based on my experience in corporate finance, I knew that with the amount of funds we were trying to raise, and the relative early stage of our company (eighteen months), we definitely needed to enlist a top-notch investment bank that would bring with them the credibility and advice that our young company could leverage.

I contacted Israel's leading investment bank, Poalim Capital Markets, and engaged them and their U.S. counterpart, William Blair, to help us raise this capital. We now had two extremely reputable and proficient investment bankers who could warmly introduce us to all of the private-equity firms in the United States. Perfect.

Before we started, I made one thing clear to them: We didn't want just capital, we wanted smart capital. We wanted investment partners who were going to be able to give us money and also help guide us through the minefield of growing a business in America. We needed hands-on partners who would be able to get actively involved in the business and help us do basic things such as establish a headquarters in the United States, introduce us to our new retailers, and tell us what not to do as much as what to do.

Poalim and William Blair did a great job and put Ido and me in front of several potential investors. We went on trips across the United States to meet and pitch up to four private-equity firms a day. I knew we had a great story to tell and our PowerPoint slides said it all:

- Emerging consumer brand in high-growth natural-product sector.
- Proven sales in major retailer.
- Multiple retailers lining up for distribution.
- Capital needed for expansion and growth needs.

It was exactly what ticked all the boxes at private-equity firms that were, at the time, brimming with cash to invest.

After only three months of pitching, we received six term-sheet offers to invest in the company. We took all of them very seriously, but one of them stood out from the others. It was from two firms, San Francisco Equity Partners, led by Scott Potter, and Simon Equity Partners, led by Steve Simon.

Ido: About six months earlier, Lance and I had traveled to Tampa Bay in Florida for the inaugural launch of Yes To on the Home Shopping Channel. It was an exhilarating time. I was about to do twelve shows in twenty-four hours to market and sell a set of Yes To Carrots products. My segments were going to be broadcast to 90 million households. Lance and I decided to visit a Target as Lance had never been to one in the States before. I took him over to an aisle in the home-cleaning products section and showed him a brand called Method.

"What do you think of these guys?" I said.

"It's an awesome brand," Lance said. "I love how they make cleaning products natural and sexy!" He thought a bit more: "They must be owned by a multinational conglomerate, considering how many products they have in Target."

"Actually, this brand was started by two guys in San Francisco, Eric Ryan and Adam Lowry, just five years ago. This is what we want to be in a couple of years: the Method of natural beauty."

Lance: So, six months later, when I went through the term-sheet offers on the table, the offer from Scott and Steve stood out.

"I don't remember pitching to these guys. Is this the one you did by yourself in San Francisco?"

Their term sheet was strong but it was not the highest offer in terms of valuation of the company. Ido looked at me with a smile; I could see he was clearly delighted that these guys had submitted a term sheet.

"They are the investors behind Method!"

I was interested, but I told Ido that if we were going to consider these guys, I first wanted to meet them face-to-face. A few days later, we flew out to San Francisco to meet Scott and Steve. Part of the point of the trip was to scope out potential new homes for Yes To; after all, we needed a new place to headquarter Yes To in the United States, and we wanted it to be close to our potential investors as well.

Scott had organized a dinner at his place on our first night in town. We arrived at his beautiful home in the suburban woods of San Francisco. His wife, Dara, had organic vegetables slow-cooking in the Crock-Pot, with sustainably caught salmon on the grill and a quinoa salad on the rough-hewn oak table. Very San Francisco. Very on-brand.

The evening was going well. Scott had said all the right things and Ido and I were growing more and more interested in the idea of partnering with him and setting up in San Francisco. I excused myself to use the bathroom, and Scott pointed me upstairs. As I headed up, I admired Scott's magnificent home and turned my attention to the artwork. One piece of art on the wall caught my attention. I looked closer, almost in disbelief—it was a painting of last year's Manchester United soccer team!

C'mon, I said to myself. This can't be true. I knew that some private-equity guys would go to some pretty crazy extremes in order to win highly desired deals. But to pretend that you love Man United enough to have a painting of them in your home? I was sure that most Americans didn't even know what Manchester United was! And how would Scott even know that I'm a Man United fanatic? This was weird —in fact, borderline creepy. I decided to go downstairs and call him out.

"Scott!" I said. "How come you have a Manchester United painting on your wall?"

"I'm a diehard supporter!" Scott replied. "Why, do you like them?"

It turned out that Scott played college soccer for Berkeley and had followed Man United his whole life. I looked at Scott with starry eyes and threw my arms around him in a hug.

"You have no idea what this means to me, Scott. No idea!"

The rest is history. Lance had made his mind up, and once Ido and the rest of our shareholders agreed, Scott and Steve became our new investment partners. We decided that in order to maximize the benefit of working with them, we would need to be geographically close, and we were easily convinced that San Francisco was the place for this. We would relocate the head office of Yes To to San Francisco, and both of us would move with our families and set up once and for all on the West Coast.

We signed and closed the deal with Scott and Steve in June 2008, raising $14 million for Yes To, a company that was less than eighteen months old. Just four months later the world's financial markets imploded and the latest recession sank in. Once again we had raised the money in the nick of time.

Years later, we asked Scott (over a great dinner and a bottle of organic Willamette Valley Pinot) what his impressions of us had been. Yes, this reads as a bit of a pat on the back, but we thought his answers were also an extremely astute summation of what business investors are looking for these days. See if anything here applies to you and your venture:

Scott: My firm had a very successful investment in Method. We believed that in order to develop a meaningful natural brand in large consumer categories, you needed to "architect" the brand in a way that appeals to the mainstream consumer. This meant that you couldn't take the traditional "hippie" brands that were developed in the natural channel (such as Whole Foods) and put them on the shelf at mass retailers like Target, Walmart, and grocery stores and expect the mainstream consumer to be willing to pay more for a product that typically didn't work as well as the traditional, nonnatural alternative.

Ido and Lance understood this concept from the very beginning and specially architected the Yes To brand to be about positive attributes like efficacious formulations, clear consumer benefits, cool packaging, great value, whimsical and fun voice, and, last but not least, natural ingredients. Simply put, Ido and Lance set out to build a mass beauty brand that happened to be natural, versus a natural brand playing in beauty. This is not an insignificant nuance!

The guys approach business in a way that lends itself to deep relationships that go beyond a typical business relationship. They have a truly unique capability, each in his own way, of connecting with people on a very meaningful level. They manage to do this in a way that strengthens the business relationship rather than having the personal side interfere with the business side.

Ido and Lance always knew what they didn't know and weren't afraid to get help when they needed it from people who had done it before. This ability to step back and really ask what your business needs at various stages of growth and what external resources you need to surround yourself with in order to provide it is key.

8

<hr>

The Nuts and Bolts of
Getting People to Care

B Y 2009, THINGS HAD STABILIZED at Yes To and we decided to initiate a brand study. We picked a brand agency called Tattoo, otherwise known in our office as Vishwa the Magnificent. Vishwa and his team are an iconic San Fran brand agency that has done brand studies and reformations for huge brands such as La Perla, Porsche, and for Oprah Winfrey.

We wanted to do the study because we realized that things were starting to click but we didn't know exactly why. We'd done everything up to that point based on our gut instincts (although we'd also ignored those instincts, to our peril). We realized that in order to solidify our relationship with our customers, we needed to understand them better. What was really going on in our customers' subconscious minds? If we understood that relationship better, would we be able to further improve our relationship with them?

Lance: A mentor of mine sold his hair-care company to Wella for $400 million. I showed him the first run of Yes To products and asked him for some general advice.

"Nice packaging," he said, "but the first thing you should do when you've raised a lot more capital is hire the best brand agency you can afford and let them do a study on precisely why your brand works. Because believe me, whatever you're thinking is probably miles off from what is actually happening." We took his advice, and he ended up being dead right. Thanks, Malcolm!

We needed to understand the fine points of what made our brand tick, so we would know how to correctly allocate our marketing budget and in what direction to take Yes To in the future.

We worked with Vishwa and his team for almost six months on our brand study. This was the single biggest effort we'd ever made to understand our customer; it involved many different types of consumer studies. We would tail customers in stores across the country, watch them when they were about to purchase Yes To, and interview them once they'd done so. We even did bathroom studies with randomly selected women, just to see how they displayed their products and to glean what they thought and how they felt about them.

Branded!

Three main things came out of the brand study, and the first was a huge surprise for us. We had been putting the marketing emphasis on the veggies and had spent $100,000 trademarking the carrot, but what people actually liked was the Yes. People liked the cuteness of the vegetable, but it confused them a little. Were we somehow a vegetarian brand? Did the product smell of carrots? Were the other vegetable products just different flavors?

So this simple tweak in value, from veggie to Yes, completely changed our look and our strategy.

One of Vishwa's goals was to summarize who we were and what we were about in a few phrases. He came up with:

- Relentless optimism
- Happy-go-lucky views
- Deliciously nourishing, wholesome feeling

We wanted to be about positivity and not be taken too seriously. Yet at the same time, we never wanted to lose sight of our "natural" credentials.

Lance: After the Tattoo study, we received our major brand points. We took these points and gave them to a design agency, and after many months their best designers came back with five major concepts — logos. Now, the problem wasn't that these ideas were off-brand. We were OK with making a change and evolving the brand, but the new logos no longer looked like Yes To. We wanted a new look and feel that was the equivalent of going from the original iPod to the iPod touch. We still wanted to be recognizable as the same brand. We wanted an evolution, not a revolution. But the way they had put it together made Yes To look like something completely different.

In short, it was the Jennifer Grey of rebrandings: the same product made unrecognizable.

Ido came to me with the pitch deck flagged by our new VP of marketing. A lot of time had elapsed over the course of the branding exercise, and costs for the project were starting to get out of control. I could see that Ido was unhappy with something, but our VP was doing her best to get him excited about the new logo and branding options. I could see Ido was not satisfied, but I wasn't sure if it was just him. As an exercise he sat down and tried to give me the pitch that our VP had given him. After listening for a few minutes, I said, "Ido, this is terrible."

"I know," he said. "We aren't doing this."

Note: When you are being pitched any radical or "big" idea for you or your company, always try "re-pitching" the idea to your partner, a smart friend, or just your dog. Does it still make sense? This is a fantastic way to figure out if the idea you're being sold actually has any value.

Ido: We went straight back to the agency and gave them the "it's not you, it's me" speech. We weren't breaking up, but we needed a change and we needed their A game, and quick! A few weeks later, they called us back for another pitch. I dreaded that meeting; I wasn't feeling hopeful, considering how off they were the last time. I walked in and saw them smiling. They knew they had come up with something awesome. Their new logo was an "evolution, not a revolution." It invoked our brand values, positive vibe, and happy-go-lucky appeal. It was perfect!

The Two Best Spends to Understand Your Brand and Your Customer

The best Big Spend you can make is a consumer study. At some stage, probably after you've been in business for a few years, you really need to understand your consumers' purchase decisions—why they do what they do, at a subconscious level. You have to figure out what your brand means to people. If you don't truly get what makes you special to your customers, you'll never be able to grow. A great branding agency can find a seemingly tiny misunderstanding that can make a big difference in the way you present and sell your brand once it's fixed.

Vishwa showed us that we weren't off base, but that we needed to tweak a few little things that cost almost nothing. These tweaks ended up improving our business by 10 percent to 20 percent.

The best Small Spend you will ever make is to trademark your name and buy the domain name. One of my friends was working on a book; the title changed six times before it went to market, and he bought every single domain name as soon as the publisher suggested it. Why? Because he knew he couldn't take the chance of not owning the domain name for his own book.

If you haven't already bought the domain name for your company, even if it's just an idea, put this book down, get out your credit card, and buy your domain name, already! It'll cost you less than fifteen dollars and save thousands if it prevents someone from buying your domain name and holding out for a big payday from the logical owner — you!

How do we know this? Because we were held hostage by a savvy American tourist who bought one of the very first bottles of Yes To Carrots in Israel, recognized the brand's potential, and immediately bought the domain name. (In case you're thinking, "How could Ido be so stupid!" this was one of the original developer's mistakes, not ours.)

We ended up paying a ridiculous price just for the right to use our own name as a Web address.

Having a great website and a terrific branding and PR campaign will help you reach your end customer, but this is just one of the amazing sales jobs you have to do to shift product. You have to sell your product *twice:* once to your end customer through marketing and advertising, and once to your retail outlets through trade shows and sales meetings. As you've heard, we've made many mistakes trying to reach our end customers, but luckily, when it came to selling to our retailers, we've been pretty great right off the bat.

Three Days of Heart-Stopping, Adrenalin-Pumping, All-Night-Partying Action: Trade Shows

Ido: There are many reasons why people start a brand or choose a career. One very good reason is to enter an industry where you have access to really awesome people. If you're going to work like crazy, at least work like crazy in an industry that will take you all over the world and give you a chance to make friends with exciting and glamorous people (like us).

Since starting Yes To, we've been invited to conferences all over the world. In the last few years, we've been everywhere — from Sydney to Prague to Palm Beach — to talk about Yes To. We've spent a week on a cruise ship in the most glamorous ports of the Caribbean and weekends in Val d'Isère. Nice work if you can get it.

Of course, all this traveling and schmoozing has a purpose: spreading the word about natural beauty, and specifically about our little natural-beauty baby, Yes To. The most important way to do this is to attend the major beauty, health, and lifestyle trade shows around the world.

We love trade shows. By "love," we mean "lose lots of sleep and obsess over them for weeks beforehand, think about them nonstop, change our outfits a dozen times beforehand, and bore our friends and coworkers to death analyzing every moment of 'he said, she said' once we finally get home." So it's love, but not always the healthiest kind of love.

Trade shows are critical for a small company with a brief window of opportunity (and a limited amount of cash) to make people care. Everyone you need to know, be it a potential buyer or a potential competitor, is trapped in the same room with you for three or four days. If you're clever and bold, you can make friends, sales, and connections. Don't be discouraged by the size of your company or the current (and temporary) reality of your business. Trade shows are at least partly a performance. You are selling yourself — enthusiastic, personable, reliable, and unique — as much as you are selling a product line.

Who you are is less important than who you are perceived to be. Providing you are honest about your products and don't write an order that you know you can't fill, it is 100 percent fine to give the most idealized and best possible version of you, your company, and your product.

Trade shows are all about presentation and about giving trade show attendees a reason to stop and check out your booth. From the get-go we were determined to stand out from the crowd. As a result, we've had "shot girls" dispensing test-tube-sized shots of carrot juice to passersby. We always have beanbags, low tables, and an unofficial "no-pressure" zone where attendees can relax for a few minutes without having to talk business or pretend to be interested in our products. This is a purposeful decision. We are more than happy to give away gallons of organic (i.e., quite expensive) carrot juice or thousands of samples to people who are never going to buy our product. We always want our booth to look like the happening spot. It's a party in row C. Which of course means that, eventually, the people we *do* want to talk to are sitting on the beanbags, sipping their shots.

The number one trick at a trade show is to stand out and be different. We were often the smallest company at these conferences, but we got disproportionate amounts of attention because we stood out in the crowds. Once again, it's all about perception when it comes to trade shows. You will never be able to outdo your multinational competitors when it comes to traditional advertising such as TV and print, but a trade show is the one time you can outshine them in front of the most important people in retail. In fact, the big guys tend to be pretty cheap when it comes to trade shows; they are there only because they have to be and they are less invested in making an impression. So they recycle the same junky trade show booths and ship them around the country, and even the world, every year.

The number two trick is to be superhuman, or at least figure out some other way to go without sleep, sunshine, fresh air, or meaningful nutrition for a week. Trade shows are astonishingly hard work. Standing around and talking shouldn't be this brutal, but you will go to bed so bone-crushingly exhausted that you'll seriously doubt you can get out of bed the next morning. There is no better opportunity to meet with the industry leaders and most influential people in retail than at a trade show. And most of them are there to have some fun as well as meet suppliers!

Lance: I actually perfected a sleep-maximization strategy I call "getting out of bed six minutes before the convention hall doors open," but I've yet to convince Ido of its usefulness. Try to avoid working a trade show with Ido if you are going to implement this approach.

The Yes To Manifesto on Making Trade Shows Work for You

Here is everything we know about how to extract the most value from a trade show. Keep in mind that we threw together our first U.S. trade show booth with nothing but hope, good vibes, a modest budget, and a fortuitous Google search that led us to an amazing design firm in Israel and a builder in Hungary who were able to build our booth for pennies on the dollar. Trade shows are absurdly expensive; save money on everything but don't skimp on your visual presentation. Sleep underneath the registration table. Eat nothing but stale pretzels. Shave in the McDonald's bathroom. But make sure that your booth looks fun, deluxe, well designed, and tells a compelling story. You need it to catch buyers' eyes as they run past you to the established businesses in the primo spots on the convention floor.

Trade shows are an incredibly useful weapon to get introductions to massive retailers, and no matter how much you think you know about international retail, there are always going to be retailers out there that you've never heard of and whose stores you need to be in.

So give it your all.

Presentation is everything.

Ido: When we first started Yes To we would attend the National Association of Chain Drug Stores convention in San Diego every year. It's a huge deal; literally everyone who is anyone in health and beauty is there. We always had the same spot, year after year; and so did the guy a few booths down from us. Now, I admired our neighbor's products. They were well formulated and effective. But I struggled to understand his approach to selling these products. Every year he had the same collapsible table, covered in the same tablecloth, with a drop-down backdrop showcasing his products. He wore a slightly scruffy suit and stood morosely at his table, rarely engaging with anyone he didn't already know. In other words, he had a great product and a terrible presentation; his table looked cheap, he seemed uninterested, and no one was going to fall in love with cheap and uninterested.

You don't need ridiculous amounts of money to make an impact, but if you're working with a minimal budget, you need to brings tons of imagination and effort and add something unique to your presentation. Don't go with a little table and a pull-down sign at the back. You don't need to spend a lot of money — just be different.

The Taj Mahal booth.

Ido: What do we mean by different? We mean *be bloody different.* A few months after we shook hands with Walgreens on our online exclusive, I went to an industry conference in Hong Kong called the Cosmoprof convention. I'd squeezed Lance for about 200 percent more money than he thought we could afford; it was still a miniscule budget by the standards of a big trade show. We'd found an architect in Israel who designed a fantastic, modern, über-hip booth for us and the aforementioned builders in Hungary who were willing to build it for a fourth of the cost of Israeli contractors.

Nobody knew anything about us except that we were the brand-new company with the over-the-top, bright orange, sexy booth. The booth had a carrot structure that rose like an orange Taj Mahal over the rest of the exhibitors. The green fronds brushed the ceiling and could be seen from any point on the floor. We filled it with energetic young people, glowing with good health, who handed moisturizer samples and carrot juice to everyone who walked by. Basically, we were the party booth, and we were packed from morning to night. Turns out that our structure was ten feet too high and broke every rule of the convention center, but we managed to stall the demolition team till the last day. By the time the convention wrapped, we'd drunk our own weight in carrot juice many times over, but we'd also made hundreds of new friends and new contacts. Success.

Now when we attend conferences we do it with an even more fantastic booth than we had at the last event. Other companies recycle their booths for decades. What's fun about that! Sometimes the booth will have a Frank Lloyd Wright look to it, other times it will be futuristic, but it is always big, orange, and fun. No matter what, our booth changes every year and is always the one that people are talking about on the opening day of the convention.

A first impression is always going to be the most lasting impression. There is a certain expectation that your booth and your presentation will reflect the reality of your business's size and market share. This is an expectation that we chose to ignore. Our booth reflected the company we planned to be in a few years, not the company we were at that moment.

So you don't need the biggest booth or the biggest budget. But at the same time, you can't simply follow the norm of having a plasma screen playing a generic video or hosting a random giveaway or competition. By the end of a trade show, people want two things:

- They want to be entertained.
- They want free stuff.

If you can make them laugh *and* send them home with a bag of goodies, then you have a reasonable chance of getting them to remember you.

Think of a trade show as speed dating on a massive level. Every account in that convention hall has the opportunity to sit down with

Lance in our first office in San Francisco, 2009. Even entrepreneurs need a little downtime on the job.

Lance, Joy and Ido: the Three Amigos. We were so excited and relieved to have Joy join the family in December 2009.   *(Yes To Inc.)*

Posing for our holiday card (notice who has the horns),
Tel Aviv, Israel, 2008.   *(Jacob Mehager)*

Ido cooking up a storm at the press launch of Yes To Cucumbers in
Paris, France, 2011.   *(Yes To Inc.)*

Not your average kitchen. This is how meals are prepared for the hundreds of children who attended Maai Mahiu Primary School. Each child must bring wood to fuel the fires that cook the meals. *(Hunter Holder)*

Exploring the Yes To Hope microfarm in Maai Mahiu, Kenya, with the incredible kids who will benefit from the nutritious and delicious veggies, 2013. *(Hunter Holder)*

Work hard, board hard. Our annual pilgrimage to the snow proves to
us that we are still twenty-one at heart, no matter what our passports say.
Whistler, Canada, February 2013.

Supporting our friends at TOMS Shoes during the company's annual One Day
Without Shoes campaign, 2011.   *(Yes To Inc.)*

every buyer for three minutes. In those 180 seconds you need to find some way to click with them, make them laugh, give them an insight into your brand's philosophy, put some samples in their hands, offer them a carrot juice and a key ring, and hope and pray that they felt the same little spark that you did.

It always shocks us when we see brands not putting a 150 percent effort into a trade show. I feel personally offended when I see attendees sitting down and reading the paper or sneaking out early. What's the point? Attending a trade show is a massive investment, especially if you're a small company with a modest budget. Don't slack off even when you see your competitors half-assing it. In fact, look at their half-assing as an opportunity for you to wow the retailers they are underwhelming.

The Master's Degree of Trade Shows: Working the Show

Lance: In our early days with Yes To we made a huge effort to attend the Cosmoprof convention in Italy. This was a biggie, and we put down a huge amount of cash to fly our team out, assemble gift bags, and make our booth look fantastic. By the end of day two, though, our booth was quiet; all the good-looking carrots, handing out juice, and the team couldn't get people interested. For whatever reason our magic wasn't clicking.

"What the hell are we going to do?" I wondered. "This is a disaster."

"Why?" Ido asked.

"Because our booth is empty, and it's been empty all day!"

Ido laughed.

"Mate, we built this booth to meet one person, from one account. I've met him, he loves us, and nothing else matters."

Have goals. Be strategic. Know whom you need to meet and what kind of business you need to do with them. Identify your "whales," the most important people you want to meet at a trade show. It's critical that your team knows the names (and ideally the faces) of the whales on your hit list. Make sure they understand that if Mr. or Ms. Whale shows up, then they need to get your attention immediately.

Trade shows are full of perfectly charming people who are lots of fun but essentially irrelevant to your business. If you are talking to one of these people, and you miss your chance to talk to the whale, then you are in trouble.

Ido: I've shamelessly run after a whale that got away; Captain Ahab would be proud of me! After all, this might be the only day your particular Moby Dick attends the trade show. Do not miss your opportunity to talk with them.

Manifesto Rule Numero Uno: Turn the convention hall into a walking billboard about you and your brand.

Conventioneers love tote bags. Why? Because there are tons and tons of free stuff to be had, and after about two hours they are going to need something to carry the swag in. We always order thousands of great tote bags. No cheap paper or thin cotton for us. Our bags are big, bright, and unique, and by day two we try to make sure that every single person in the hall is carrying one. Be shameless and be fun. Slap your logo on the bag, add some bright colors, and make sure that people instinctively smile when they see it.

Have tons of product to give away at the booth, and give it away freely. Don't be one of those guys withholding the good stuff for the "big guys." Instead, be the guy with the product that everyone is using and talking about. Freely distributing swag (even if it costs you) is in your best interests; you want those walking adverts wandering the convention.

Try to stay in the hotel where the important people are staying, because you want to be able to interact with them in the elevator, in the bar, or at breakfast. A two-minute conversation in the breakfast buffet line can be invaluable if it creates a tiny bond or shared experience between you and an important buyer. Give yourself the chance to have that moment. These hotels are expensive, but it is so, so worth the extra cost if you are able to use it to your advantage.

Always make sure you and your team have a uniform — and not a suit. Order some logo shirts, but make sure they are funny, not drone-y. Do something goofy and unexpected. Order everyone in the team those East Coast preppie trousers that are covered with embroidered whales. Have fun with it, but whatever you come up with, make sure it makes you stand out. You want to be a little bit different and also be comfortable, so don't wear a corporate, uninviting suit. One caveat: It's useful to have someone who looks more conventional in your booth. Some of your meetings will be with a person who needs the reassurance of seeing someone who looks a little square.

Lance: At every damn trade show Ido sees me putting on my jeans and polo shirt and says, "I'm dressing cool, you dress like the accountant."

Ido: That's just because of your terrible taste in jeans. No, we need one guy who looks serious and traditional, and seriousness comes more naturally to Lance.

Note: The more conventional, reserved-looking guy should not be the boss or, in our case, both of the bosses. Make sure that at least one of the founders or the CEO is wearing the more casual look, like everyone else. You want your CEO or founder to be fun and super-approachable. You don't want him or her wearing a suit and sitting in one spot and looking like a monarch on a throne. Keep the boss approachable, and don't create the impression that you have an impenetrable hierarchy. Buyers buy from people they know, like, and trust. Give them a chance to build that relationship with the head guy, even if it is the one and only time they will ever have anything to do with him.

Always have a pen and paper, or an iPad, or a voice recorder handy. As soon as you finish a meeting, scribble down all the pertinent information: name, contact info, and any details you can recall. Small talk is everything, and six months later you may be glad you remembered that their youngest is playing ball at State, or that they grew up in an area you know well.

Send a follow-up note to everyone you contacted over the course of the day, and every evening debrief with your team so you figure out who to delegate your new contact to. Keep the initial note brief; no one has the time or energy to read a detailed letter while the show is still running.

Once you are back home, give them a couple of days to settle back and then hit them again with an action-based e-mail. Always remind them who you are, and refer back to your notes. If you have a personal comment that feels appropriate, such as, "I hope John's first day of school went well," make it.

Know how to cut your losses; if someone says, "I am coming back," without scheduling an actual time to return and talk, it means they are never coming back, ever. Let it go.

The minute the trade show closes for the day is the minute the real work begins.

Practice the fine art of thinking while drinking.

Lots of the important business at a trade show is done after the convention closes for the day. In order to get in on these opportunities, you need to be organized, aggressive, and targeted.

Plan ahead. You want at least one after-hours social interaction with all your potential partners, retailers, distributors, press, and even your competitors. You need to start planning these social interactions months before the convention, so start calling and e-mailing and Facebooking well in advance of the show. Don't be afraid to approach people whom you've never met or who feel "out of your league." Everyone is in the same boat of wanting to connect with people and discover the next big idea before their competitors do. This makes it relatively easy to get a meeting at a convention that you might struggle to get in day-to-day life.

You are at that convention to build relationships and make friends, and the after-hours booze fest known as "cocktail hour" is a great place to do so. For better or worse, conventions are fueled by alcohol; this can be challenging if you don't drink, but either way, it's critical to be out there taking part.

Conventions, especially the after-parties, can also be tricky if you're not a naturally outgoing person. I have friends and coworkers who are great in the more structured environment of the convention floor but struggle with the after-hours socializing. It's critical that you are genuine, relaxed, and unguarded, so find something about the evening that you enjoy. Go to karaoke. Laugh. Have fun.

Say yes to after-dinner drinks and late-night drinks; late-night drinks is where you can form the strongest relationships. People are relaxed, they open up a bit, and you will have a really memorable shared experience to refer back to as your relationship develops.

Lance: Ido and I never sit together at these after-hours events. We spend plenty of time together as it is! You should chat and catch up with your partner only when you go back to your room to debrief. These after-dinner and late-night drinks are work, and we stick to our divide-and-conquer strategy.

If I had a huge ego, this would be a problem, but the reality is that there is room for only one star, and in this setting the star is Ido. In this business you have to put away your feelings of insecurity. You don't need to show them, particularly when you are trying to sell an aspirational brand. So I'm cool with Ido having the spotlight, and I use my time most effectively in supporting him as he makes these connections with the major players. At the end of the day, we both end up winning.

Be the most noticeable guy in the room.

If you have a key account coming to a trade show, do whatever it takes to have him or her to yourself for the night. Don't book the best restaurant in town. Book the most fun restaurant in town. The dinner is not about spreadsheets and marketing plans; it's about eating great food, drinking plenty of great wine (or, in the case of some of our most "fun" accounts, getting blasted on shots of Jägermeister), and truly becoming friends with people whom you generally do not get to see outside of a corporate setting.

There are going to be a few meetings that are a tougher "get," and these are generally the very biggest companies at the show. If you're struggling to get a meeting with them, ask around and find out if they are throwing a party. Yes? Great! Go and have fun and shake some hands. This is an infallible strategy — if you're invited! If you aren't invited, then you need to worm your way onto the guest list. The more exclusive the party, the more important it is to attend. So here's our crash course in, well, crashing.

1. Ask your neighbors and customers what they are doing that evening; identify the big-ticket party for that night. Are you on the list? No? Then get working!

2. Find the best-looking and most genuinely charming guy or girl from your booth. Brief them on their objective and send them off to infiltrate the booth of the company hosting the party. Arm them with free samples and big smiles.

3. If that doesn't work, find out where the party is, dress up, and tag along with a few other people that you know were invited and behave as though you own the joint (works 95 percent of the time). Effusively shake the host's hand and thank him

or her for the invite. Now that you've been such a mensch,* there's no way they can kick you out!

4.   Party like they are throwing the event just for you! Don't act like a fool, but make sure everyone at the event knows that you are the life of the party.

5.   Convince your most important suppliers/friends/staff to join you for after-party drinks at the bar in their hotel.

6.   Look at your watch and realize that the conference floor opens in forty-five minutes! Run up to your room. Do fifty push-ups and drink three coffees.

7.   Repeat every night till you are ready to cry with exhaustion.

8.   Go home!

Treat your booth with love, and it will love you back.

First, make sure you have lots of products to swap at the end of the show! Your spouse/partner/roommate will be very happy because you can barter your stuff for other people's stuff. Second, all convention-eers love getting products for free or in a barter. They'll give it to their friends, or even better, give it to their family members, and there is nothing more effective than a buyer's family liking the product.

Most trade shows end in the early afternoon of the last day, and most trade show rules stipulate that all attendees keep their booths fully open till the very last minute of the last day of the trade show. But that last day is hard; you're exhausted, and all you want to do is go home and sleep. You suddenly realize that consuming nothing but coffee and pretzels for four days is a questionable idea. By noon the convention floor is almost empty, with only a few people running around to wrap up last-minute deals. The temptation to put up your "closed" sign and slip some teamsters $500 to make your booth go away is HUGE.

---

* gentleman

Don't do it.

As much as you may be sick of the sight of your booth by the end of an event, always treat it with respect. Remember that you are going to want to use parts of it again, so don't just hand over the job of tearing it down to a couple of guys loitering around the coffee stand.

Always make sure you know who is going to pull the booth down and where it is going to go. Make sure your original builder has supplied some kind of plan for safely packing and shipping the booth. We ended up flying two men over from Hungary to pull down our first booth; we reckoned that the additional investment was worth it if it improved our odds of still having a beautiful booth for the next trade show.

Third, and equally important, squeeze every drop of value out of that show. The last day is generally quieter and slower and you never really know who might show up at the booth. If the last day is very quiet, it can be a good time to start following up on the people you and your team met during the show. Make sure you speak to the show organizers to secure you the same or a better location for your booth for next year. (If you forget to do this, you may end up wedged in between the line for the toilets and the rubbishy food outlets. Not good.)

The Multibooth Philosophy

After a show, our booth is shipped back to a storage facility, which is a little like the government warehouse in *Raiders of the Lost Ark*. We have various booths in storage crated up and ready to go. Our philosophy is to never show the same booth twice at the same convention or trade show. For example, the Taj Mahal Carrot will never go back to Hong Kong, but it will do very well at Las Vegas. The goal is to keep things surprising and fresh. You want people to be curious about what you've done differently from last time, and by rotating the booths we maximize the chances of our important accounts seeing something new every year.

You may not have the budget for this; if that's the case, then get creative. Keep the same basic shell, the same colors and overall design philosophy, but change things up a little. Have fun, but make sure your aesthetics align over the years. You want to surprise people, not confuse them.

Getting people excited about Yes To was the easy part. The hard part was everything else! Even while we were circling the world on the Trade Show Express, we had to deal with the nuts and bolts of actually manufacturing and shipping ever-increasing amounts of product.

Now, remember how we talked about how partners have to work well together, in good times and bad? Another one of those bad times is coming up right now.

9

The Most Screwed-up Screw-up

THE BIGGER YOU GET, THE more people become involved in your success, or lack thereof. This is a good and a bad thing. Your company is growing — great! On the potentially problematic flip side, you will no longer be able to directly oversee all aspects of your business. Little mistakes will be made, and if you aren't there to catch them in time, these mistakes can grow exponentially until your tiny screw-up is big enough to potentially kill your company.

Yes To's biggest and scariest screw-up happened in the spring of 2009. Ironically, it was a great moment for our business. After all the hard work and setbacks, Yes To was slowly taking off. We were out of exclusivity with Walgreens and were now being stocked in Target, Duane Reade, and elsewhere. One of our biggest retailer wins had come with the signing and launch of an exclusive European distribution deal with Sephora Europe that meant they were stocking us in fifteen countries. It was a deal that had been a long time in the making and secured directly with Sephora's then CEO and legendary leader, Jacques Levy.

Things were going very well and our confidence was sky-high.

In fact, we sometimes felt like we had the Midas touch. The United States was going through a massive recession, but we were succeeding despite that. We were winning new customers because women were trading down from premium natural-beauty brands to more mainstream naturals. At the same time, our customers weren't going "down a rung" in the same way; they were unwilling to trade down to petroleum-based products. The recession worked for our niche because we offered a better price for a staple item. This gave our existing customers a reason to stay loyal, but it also offered our new customers more value than they were used to.

Ido: Ronit and I had decided to take a long-delayed and much-needed vacation in Tel Aviv. Leaving Lance in charge, we jumped on a plane for two weeks of sunshine and relaxation. The relaxation lasted till about three minutes after we'd landed, when the flight attendants announced it was safe to turn our cell phones back on. I grabbed my iPhone and listened to the first of eight messages from my office in Israel saying, "Call us. It's an emergency."

By the time the 747 was at the gate, I had been filled in on the awful details. One of our new manufacturers had called Lance to let him know that there might be a quality-control issue with a preservative in one of our products. This manufacturer had fulfilled orders for our Sephora account, and it was possible that some of the potentially tainted stock had already been shipped. Too many mights, possiblys, and perhapses. The truth was, nobody was sure what kind of a problem this was—a mega screw-up, a modest screw-up, or a minor one?

Lance: We have always had a very strict system of quality control; like any beauty brand, we test every batch of product before it gets shipped. We had signed our contract with Sephora shortly before this and subsequently had signed a contract with a new manufacturer to help fulfill the order. This new supplementary stock was the problem. One of our managers went into the warehouse where we were holding the shipment, did a routine batch test, and noticed that the preservative system had started to fail in one of the products. Instead of being pure and white, the product looked like an oxidizing apple. The moisturizer was turning brown, it looked horrible, and it was something we would never want customers to open up the product and see.

Now, as we all know, stuff happens. I'm pretty sure that we aren't the first beauty brand to test a bottle of product, preshipment, and see that there was a minor potential problem with it. I'm even going to guess that some brands might do some quick risk analysis, decide to roll the dice, and ship the product without saying anything. After all, it's more than possible that (a) the product wouldn't fail, and (b) if it did fail, the end consumer who bought the compromised product would just throw it away. The product that was already on shelves in Sephora was a mix of new product from the new manufacturer and old product from the older producer. The older product was fine, and we could potentially fly under the radar and cross our fingers.

So we could hope for the best and take a chance on a good outcome, or we could go straight to Sephora, say we have concerns because of a batch check, and tell them there might be a need for a recall. It took about sixty seconds of discussion to realize that we had to come clean, no matter what the eventual cost for us and the brand.

Ido: As Lance and I talked over the options, I felt my good spirits evaporate. I was almost instantly inconsolable. All I could see was our natural-beauty baby dying in front of us. I turned to Ronit.

"Babe," I said, "I'm sorry, have fun, I'm going to Paris, you're on your own." And because she's amazing, she didn't say anything much more than "Good luck, I love you." I grabbed a taxi and ran straight to the El Al ticket desk and booked a seat on the next flight to Paris. I had no particular plan beyond an urgent realization that I needed to get to Sephora's head office and talk this over in person. As I said earlier, we believe in the power of face-to-face conversation rather than a phone call, e-mail, or text for good news or bad. And this was very bad news. There was no way I was discussing this over the phone.

Four hours and one very expensive last-minute plane ticket later, I was in Paris. I called up Jacques Levy and told him I was on my way, there was a product issue, and we needed to talk. When he asked where I was and I said, "Charles de Gaulle," he sounded surprised, but to this day I believe that having the following conversation face-to-face was what saved us.

I caught the Metro and very shortly found myself walking into Jacques's office, where he was sitting with another colleague. I started immediately, running through what I knew with all the maybes, mights, and perhaps. I told them that I was planning on staying in Paris until the whole issue was resolved and that I was at their beck and call till they were happy.

Jacques and his colleague are the picture of sophisticated Parisian charm, but despite their Yves Saint-Laurent exterior they know a surprisingly varied and inventive array of extremely vivid and descriptive words in two, possibly three, languages. After a while I lost count. All I could do was take it; their anger was justified and understandable. Look at it from the retailer's perspective. I'd just walked in and announced that every Sephora in the European Union was going to have fourteen inches of empty shelf space for up to six months. The math is horrifying; let's just say it adds up to an unbelievable amount of lost revenue and, equally important, empty shelves that confuse customers and are visually unsatisfying.

Finally, Jacques took a breath and said, "Ido, how are we going to solve this together?"

Lance: As soon as Ido walked out of that meeting he called me, we had a quick talk, and we decided to talk to a product-recall expert. As we explained the situation, the expert started to chuckle in a kindly way. She could hear in our voices that we were completely deflated and stressed almost to the breaking point. Finally, she interrupted us.

"Guys," she said, "we make a living out of managing product recalls because every consumer-goods company in the world deals with this situation." This is true. Any and every consumer good will have product quality issues at some point. It's not a huge or unusual problem. Our real problem was that we'd never prepared for it, so our expectations were what frightened us the most. There were so many variables that were essentially out of our control and that could kill our company.

We hung up the phone feeling completely shaken and quite morose, but at least we now had a plan.

Ido: Within a few days we had initiated a product-withdrawal protocol. All the potentially affected items were randomly tested; it would take a week to get the results back. For one week, I sat in a hotel room in Paris, too nervous to watch TV or go for a walk, just waiting for the phone to ring. We had no idea what direction this would go, what the impact would be, what the PR would be, how the news would affect our customers.

Strangely, the protocol felt almost reassuring. Even though it was terrifying, at least we were doing something. Whatever happened, we felt like we had our first foot on the slope out of the pit of despair.

The end result is that we took back every single one of the potentially affected products, tested them, and then destroyed them. By the end of it, we had trashed two million dollars' worth of product, of which 99.9 percent were fine and unaffected. We also initiated a voluntary product withdrawal that allowed customers to return products they had bought for a full refund.

The product withdrawal was hugely stressful because we were so emotionally attached to Yes To. The potential financial repercussions were crazy, but that wasn't really what was worrying us. We could make more money. What we couldn't do was find a business that we loved, and were passionate about, and meant as much to us as Yes To did. We blew up the product withdrawal in our minds to such an extent that it was like we were standing on the deck of the *Titanic* looking at the iceberg. As you know, we are all about perception, and we were convinced that our baby would be tarnished by bad publicity, unfair accusations, and general bad vibes. We were convinced that this recall would kill Yes To.

Lance: A week later we got the results back from the lab. The tests revealed that the preservative system had failed in just enough products that we were one degree from being on the "failed" side. This test was very stringent. It put the product to the toughest and most unforgiving standard: 90 percent of the product passed, 10 percent failed. Note that "failed" meant that the preservative in the product *might* fail.

Once again it came down to *might, possibly,* and *conceivably.* It's possible that nothing bad would have happened if Lance and I had kept the bad news to ourselves and never said anything to Sephora. Other companies might have handled it differently, and frankly, maybe they would have been smart to do so. There's an element of calculated risk on all sides in the business world. However, at our core we believe that you're nothing without your integrity; the way we handled the withdrawal took us from the level of a "small company" to a "small company that does the right thing." And *that's* priceless.

Lance: I'm proud of the fact that we were able to survive this event. It came at a terrible time. The United States was in a recession, and while the end consumer still loved us, the retail outlets were nervous, and some were destocking products to cut back on inventory. Even though we began the year being cash-flow positive and profitable, we ended up losing more money than in any other year. It was a million-dollar hit and one we couldn't afford, but we were able to survive.

The end result was that we received one complaint (in all of Europe) of someone who got a rash. We used the experience to improve our product-testing system. And funnily enough, the checks they did introduced a new process and protocol for all of Sephora's products.

Sephora ended up having empty shelves for nearly six months, which as we mentioned earlier turned into massive lost sales. They had already paid us, so they either wanted us to pay them back or credit us with new stock. This was (obviously) huge for us, but by now we knew we were going to survive the withdrawal.

Lance: About a year later, when we had fixed everything up and taken a multimillion-dollar charge to the business, we launched Yes To Tomatoes, Cucumbers, and Blueberries. When you are in a terrible situation it can be hard to imagine you'll ever recover; however, if you are determined, it is possible. Almost a year to the day after Ido's last (awful) meeting in Paris, we met Jacques and his team in Newport Beach to discuss expanding the new lines to an international distribution level. Jacques looked me in the eye and said, "Lance, if it wasn't for me, you guys wouldn't be around."

We are so grateful to Jacques; for his team it was just another product on the shelf, but for him it was personal, and he went above and beyond to stand by us, support us within Sephora, and give us every chance to "make this right." (Jacques passed away in 2012. He was a truly distinguished gentleman in every sense of the word, and Ido and I will eternally miss him.)

At the end of the day, performance and numbers are one thing but relationships are everything. Yes, you have to have a great product and a functional organization, but layered on top of that are the relationships you have with your vendors, your customers, and your retailers. Those relationships are never more important than when you are in trouble; they can give you a second opportunity, one you wouldn't get otherwise.

Eventually, the product manufacturer agreed to reimburse us for the product loss and all the ancillary costs that went into it, and yes, although it was difficult, we were able to keep a positive relationship with them as well.

You need to have a never-say-die attitude, even when what you want to do is crawl under your desk and disappear for a while. If you are willing to do whatever it takes to fix a problem, and the people who are relying on you see that you are willing to do whatever it takes, then you can overcome pretty much anything.

10

Putting It All Together

WHAT DOES ALL THIS EXPERIENCE boil down to? A brand lives and dies on, well, how good of a brand it is. "Good" can mean many things. Are your formulations top-notch? Do you know how to engage and excite your customer? Is your infrastructure strong, flexible, and resilient? What's your brand's philosophy, and do you live and breathe it? Are you able to build and maintain good relationships with your retailers? If we had to boil down everything we think about brand building, this would be it:

The Yes To Guide to Better Branding

Ido: Ten years ago Lance decided that he needed a really great watch. He was just starting out in the business world and this was the pre-iPhone era; if you wanted to flash a great accessory that said something about who you were, and you couldn't afford an expensive car, then you needed to have a great watch.

A few days later he walked into a café to have a coffee with me, sat down, and in typical Kalish style nonchalantly put his arm down on the table so I could get a good look at the surprisingly dainty watch adorning his wrist.

I immediately started laughing: He was clearly wearing a ladies' watch.

"What did you do, mug a twelve-year-old on her way to dance practice?"

"It's unisex!"

And we've been having the same conversation about Lance's watch ever since. He insists it's unisex; I insist that Tag Heuer doesn't make unisex watches and that the salesmen must have been pissing themselves laughing when they made the sale.

Lance: For the thousandth time, it's a *unisex watch!*

Ido: The point is . . . well, there is no point here except Lance won't admit the truth about his watch and possibly there's something there about brand loyalty occasionally being blind. But mostly the point is just about Lance being a stubborn mule.

Where were we? Building the better brand, right. Let's take a look at the first (imaginary) brand we were involved in together.

Gathering the Knowledge

A huge part of our final grades at university was earned in an elaborate business role-playing game that was staged every year. Playing the game was like reenacting the final scenes from *War Games.* A bunch of earnest, nerdy kids hovered over their computers, convinced their world would implode if they hit the wrong key. By the end we had the glazed-eyed, rumpled-suit look of the mid-level executive getting off of a twelve-hour flight after an end-of-trade-show-sake bender. So it was pretty realistic, really.

The game was a simulation of running a cola company. Every team started out with the same numbers and you get to choose the inputs, like the level of advertising, R&D, and manufacturing costs.

Now, if you're rolling your eyes, thinking, "Alright, next he's going to tell us how he rebooted the game, played some crazy strategy, and won in such a spectacular fashion that there's a bronze plaque of his pocket calculator in study hall." We *did* play crazy strategies, but the end result wasn't quite what we'd anticipated.

We didn't want to win. We wanted to WIN! In order to do so we decided we had to play a bold game. The biggest, most dramatic move we could make was to do the opposite of what we had been taught and what everyone else was doing. Rather than focus on research and development or distribution, we decided to pump ten times the recommended amount into marketing. It was a very risky strategy, but it was also the only way to explode off of the starting blocks and really distinguish ourselves among the other teams. For a few glorious weeks our share price was ten times that of our competitor. We were making huge impressions with our customers, brand awareness was through the roof! It was awesome! We had this thing sorted. How come no one else had ever thought of this? We had the largest market share and everything was great. But in the final two sessions we were forced to make four urgent decisions in a row—and suddenly our stock price crashed.

It was a pretty compelling lesson in the dangers of hubris. We were convinced we were geniuses and suddenly our share price was through the floor. We ended up winning, but rather than winning by ten or twenty times we won by a couple of pennies on our share price. It was the system's way of teaching us the lesson that there are severe consequences for high-risk maneuvers in the first stage of a company's life.

What we learned is that in order to succeed, you need to balance a hundred different inputs and outputs, along with your own preconceived notions about what you are doing and why you are doing it, plus the ever-changing realities of the evolving marketplace. Success is a mixture of doing things that have been proven to work *and* taking big chances based on your individual strengths and momentary opportunities.

So here in about fourteen steps is our guide to:

Building the Better Brand

Step One: Pick a really great name.

It's obvious but also incredibly hard to do. A great brand needs a memorable name. Apple, Virgin, Amazon, Lululemon. At face value, none of these names have any obvious relation to the products they represent. But that doesn't necessarily matter. It's more important to create something that is succinct and memorable but that can at the same time convey the emotion that your brand stands for.

So pick something really good.

Ido: As you already know, I called my first company Techtrend. No, Tradetrend. I mean Tradetech. Wait, Trendtrade! That's it. Trendtrade still exists, and I have one person working for me who has to double-check that she is calling the company by its correct name *every time she references it in a document or e-mail.* It is truly that unmemorable.

I'd like to say that she just isn't paying attention, but I suspect her complete inability to recall it could be classified as a major branding fail.

Lesson learned: If you are going to choose a horribly bad name, choose it for your first, smaller business. And try, try, try to pick a slightly better one for the business that takes off. I can't take the credit for the name Yes To, but I can take credit for absolutely refusing to allow Lance to change the name to Carrotonia.

Lance: I thought Yes To Carrots was so oversimplified that it sounded stupid, but really that simplicity was part of the brand vision that Ido had. At that time, most natural-beauty brands (and especially the brands we were representing through Trendtrade) had sophisticated-sounding "premium" names. It was really kind of groundbreaking to base our brand on such a simple name. But most times simple is best; our name is easy to recall, it's quirky, and it screams positive. Once we'd agreed on the name, I'd tell it to my friends and I'd always get the same response: They'd pause and think about it and smile. And they never forget it.

Ido: The other major attribute of the name Yes to Carrots is that it paints a very visual picture. Most people remember things as pictures, so if you can come up with a brand that people can visualize — and people put a "yes" and a fruit together very easily — they are going to remember your brand name.

Lance: It was so simple, and that's why I originally hated it — but it was the simplicity that worked.

Ido: I stuck to my beliefs that Yes To was about something else and that the name represented the positivity and passion we were bringing to this brand.

Second lesson learned: Resist any pressure to change a good name. Brands get in trouble when they decide to rebrand unnecessarily. At one point England's Royal Mail decided they needed to rebrand as a company for the future. They reckoned they needed a name that reflected their role in the modern world. Their new name? Consignia. Sounded vaguely modern and Internet-y, but it meant nothing and said nothing. Useless! The public was outraged and confused and the name was changed back within a few years.

Yes To Carrots is simultaneously a strong, iconic (hopefully), and very flexible name; chop off "Carrots" and add another fruit or veggie in its place and the name works with any other lines we add to the brand.

In 2010 we took advantage of this flexibility and formally changed the brand name to Yes To.

Step Two: Be a little bit delusional.

Now, you think we would have learned something from our imaginary cola company and made entirely smart and rational decisions ever since that moment. However, as it turns out, there is an element of self-delusion that is actually helpful when you are in the "no guts, no glory" phase of building your brand. Being a little blind to all the reasons why your business can't possibly succeed is necessary when you're starting out; otherwise, you'd never leave the house, would you?

When we started working with Yes To, we thought we were going to be three or four times as big after a few years than we actually became. Our dreams were unrealistic, but they got us motivated. The key nuance here is that it is OK to have dreams, but you have to be realistic about how you spend against those dreams. You need to be clear about what outcomes you need to achieve in order to define yourself as successful.

Ido: My dad always said, "Take photos of the things you want." It's OK to want physical things. It's OK to want a nice house, a nice car. Take those photos and put them up on the wall and visualize yourself having them. My visual cues were a little different. I knew the type of house and car I wanted, and I can tell you it has worked out, but at the same time the thing I spent the most time visualizing was the shelf space that I wanted for our brand.

We couldn't afford to buy data in our first few years of business; we were basically flying blind. We had no idea how we were performing against our competitors, which wasn't necessarily a bad thing because we weren't focusing on a number, we were just doing things. When we finally got the numbers, we found out that we were the fifth-biggest natural-beauty brand in the marketplace (and now we are number two).

Having those delusions can drive you forward, as long as you can still clearly visualize what you want for your company.

Step Three: Be a little bit jealous.

My team learns to hate me before we go to a trade show. I become obsessed. Are we going to have the best booth? Are our competitors going to make a bigger splash than we do? What are they doing? How do we measure up? Are our rivals launching new products that are going to blow me (and our accounts) away? Will there be a new brand that is just brilliant?

Inside every entrepreneur there needs to be a sixteen-year-old kid going out with his first girlfriend. You've got to be jealous. To this day I get the Target, Walmart, and Walgreens catalogs every single week; if I see a competitor advertised, I get jealous.

A little jealousy is a great motivator, just don't get too Shakespearian about it. If your new office nickname is "Othello," you've probably gone too far.

Step Four: Hold off on advertising till you really understand your product and your customer.

Lance: Over the course of this book we've told you about our experiences with some hits and some serious misfires with branding and advertising. You've heard details about the good and the bad as you read, but it can boil down to this: Hold off on a media campaign until you know exactly what you want to say and how you need to say it. You need to be crystal clear on who you are, who your customers are, what you are selling them, and how you will make them care. Hold off until you have the right advertising agency or in-house person who will sell you the ads and impressions that will actually work for you, rather than them. Don't worry that you are losing opportunities by not having an advertising presence. *Wait until all the elements are in place and you have the right ideas, the right people, and the money to do it well.*

Step Five: Don't outspend, outmaneuver.

Ido: We are *obsessive* about our competitors. When we first started out I was on Burt's Bees' website every day, trying to figure out how we could improve on what they were doing. Burt's Bees advertised on national media, and they were driving tons of people to our shelf space (generally we are placed next to each other in the naturals aisle). When we realized that, we decided that we needed to figure out how to capture the Burt's Bees customer for ourselves.

We realized that one of the easiest things we could do was get aggressive on product sizing and offer more product for the same dollar amount. And for the first two years we did aggressive price promotions. Rather than try and outspend our competitors' campaigns (since our competitors were driving the customer into our aisle), we would do "buy one, get one free" promotions and give the customer better value. By doing this we were able to level the playing field *and* piggyback on our competitors' ability to get a consumer interested in naturals. A small company has to get creative when going up against a Goliath. Look at ways that you can level the playing field by looking better on the shelf and making yourself a better buy.

Some companies believe that the only way to succeed is through something ridiculously unique. Ridiculously unique belongs in the Sky Mall catalog—if you want to create a dog's water bowl that also air-conditions your house, great! Go to Sky Mall. But if you want to sell something to the mass market, you need to do something that the customer already understands. Look at ways that you can improve on your competitors' innovations. We don't need to be the innovators when it comes to packaging.

Lance: We learned this lesson the hard way as well (are you noticing a pattern here?). One of the first Yes To Carrots products was the Hand & Nail Spa Manicure. This was an amazing, completely natural product rich with Dead Sea salts and actual pieces of organic carrots. It gave results as soon as it was applied. Customers who tried it loved it! Ido and I took bets on whether this would be our best-selling product. It was unique, an awesome experience to use, and a great value as well. I just couldn't see how people weren't going to go nuts about this product.

But in the end, the Hand & Nail Spa Manicure completely bombed. It became our bottom-selling product. Why? Simple. No one understood what in the hell it was or how to use it. You had to demonstrate the product to convince customers, but how do you do that across six thousand stores?

We learned from this experience with our eye-roller line of products. These are high-potency skin treatments that come in a pen-shaped dispenser with a small rollerball that allows the consumer to "glide" the product on in a controlled way. Brands like Garnier led the way in this category. They introduced the concept to our customer; we were then able to come in with a natural version that has become one of our most popular products. If *we'd* tried to introduce the customer to a radically new product, it probably wouldn't have worked; we just don't have pockets deep enough to get the message out.

So look at megacorporations as your potential allies; they are driving people to your shelves. Your job is to sing, tap dance, do whatever it takes to get that customer to "look at me!" instead of your competitor. **Don't outspend, outmaneuver.** Think of yourself as a little speedboat zooming around aircraft carriers, trying not to get hit.

Step Six: Realize that good ideas can come from unexpected places.

Lance: As you've probably figured out by now, Ido and I each have unique skill sets. He's great at some things and rubbish at other stuff, and so am I. But every so often one of us has a brainwave in the other's "territory." If we're smart, we put aside our egos and say, "Hey, that's an interesting idea, mate!"

Right around the time Walgreens offered us a second shelf, I started to notice that my wife, Loren, was using facial wipes all the time. By "all the time," I mean she was going through a pack of crappy wipes every week. Now, this was an interesting observation considering that I was the co-owner of a natural-beauty brand! If Loren was willing to pay almost ten dollars a week for rubbish wipes, then how would she—and other women—feel about natural, highly effective wipes at the same price point?

The next day I got Ido on the phone and excitedly told him that I'd had my "eureka" moment. For once I was the wildly enthusiastic guy telling my partner, "This is going to be huge!" As I explained my breakthrough I noticed a decided lack of enthusiasm coming back over the phone line. Which of course made me even more determined to pitch the hell out of it.

Ido: Every so often Lance has a "great" product idea. My response is always the same: "Sounds great, mate. We'll keep that on the back burner, OK?" And generally Lance goes back to his financial wizardry and twenty-four hours later he's forgotten all about it. This time was different. The next day he was on about the wipes again. And the day after. When he was still talking about the wipes a week later, I agreed to present it at our upcoming sales meeting with Target. Now, I had literally no interest in the wipes concept. We are a green, natural company. Selling a single-use, nonbiodegradable product was literally the last thing I wanted to do. But now that I had promised to present the product, I asked our manufacturers to research production. To my surprise the team came back with a wipe that was completely on-brand—biodegradable, organic, and hypoallergenic. And yes, they could start production immediately if we got sales.

When we went into the sales meeting, I presented all our upcoming products. The meeting was almost over and I could feel Lance's eyes on me. He was so excited he was practically holding his breath. It was time to talk about our newest—and at that point purely hypothetical—product. In fact, it made sense to talk about the wipes with Target; Target is renowned for encouraging innovation and moving fast with new opportunities. We had been working with them for a little over a year, but they were fast becoming our number one retailer. The Target buying team consistently challenges us to come up with new ideas and products and they are always keen to trial them. Maybe Lance was right and Target would see the brilliance in this idea.

"Oh, we have one more product to talk about," I said nonchalantly. I clicked on a mock-up of the wipe. "We are doing a line of facial wipes, and—"

The buyer put his hand up immediately.

"Ido, let me stop you right there. That's the best idea you've mentioned today. We'll take a full line of wipes."

Lance looked like he was going to explode! He was set at full-on Frank.

As soon as we got back from the meeting we went into accelerated product development for the wipes. Everything went smoothly except for the fragrance selection process. The office was evenly divided between preferring a "natural" and light fragrance or a heavier and more perfumed scent. This went on till the night before the wipes were due to start production. Finally, we gave our intern a box of sample wipes (with each scent) and told her to go down to the bar that is (conveniently) located below our office and buy pitchers of margaritas for the happy-hour crowd. Anyone who offered an opinion about which scent was better got a free drink!

Three hours later our slightly tipsy intern reported back that the crowd almost unanimously preferred the lighter scent. That's how we do crowdsourcing in San Francisco!

In the end, we pulled it off. Three months later, the Yes To Cucumbers Facial Towelettes were on shelves, and they quickly became the number one product in the entire category. Lance has had a field day with this one ever since.

My takeaway from this is: Let your partner surprise you. Listen to them when they have an idea in "your" area of expertise and give it a chance. Don't pigeonhole each other; after all, you are both see-ing, reviewing, and thinking about the same inputs and information, but from different perspectives. Be open to the possibility that your partner's perspective may occasionally be more interesting than your own!

Step Seven: Personify your brand.

Lance: Ido is famous for many things, but one of them is his wholehearted commitment to the color orange. He has orange shirts, orange shoes, and orange computer bags. You name it, he's probably worn it. Now, it's arguable that Ido might look better in a nice tomato red, or perhaps a soft cucumber green, but Yes To's original image was built around the idea of carrots, so orange it is.

Ido: The first piece of "orange" that I ever bought was the tie I wore to meet Michelle at Walgreens. That meeting went so well that I thought, "You know what, I'm going to start wearing orange every day." It started off as a joke, because I would just scour the stores for something in orange, and one of the great things about orange is that it's an unpopular color that is always on sale! Orange underwear, suits with orange linings, watches. Orange cases for iPhones. It became a way for me to remind myself about where we started and what we are about. The color orange is a happy color, it makes me stand out, and it gives people a positive impression. I am different from the rest of the crowd when I'm in orange. People look for the little glint of orange when I walk into a meeting.

There is a huge amount of competition in this industry, and you have to figure out a way to stand out in a way that works for you. I could cut my hair in a Mohawk, but it wouldn't get me the kind of at-tention I want.

Lance: I should point out that this is a metaphorical Mohawk, since Ido waved goodbye to his hair sometime in the late nineties.

Ido: The single best thing you can do on a personal level is to figure out what makes you stand out and then embrace that unique-ness with confidence. Sometimes people say, "I'm smarter and I work harder than the person who got a promotion," or "My product is bet-ter than the product that is beating me." In that case, I'd ask, "What are you doing to make yourself stand out?" The best product *doesn't always win,* and it takes more than a great idea to succeed. We see so many new brands come to conventions or trade shows and they just sit there quietly. You need to put your hand up, you need to stand out, you need to command and demand attention. If you don't have the confidence, just fake it.

We are not smarter than our peers, we just put ourselves forward more because we want it so badly. Wearing orange is a small and easy gesture; I'm not jumping out of a hot-air balloon, but my orange socks have an impact; they've become my trademark. What's yours?

Step Eight: Evaluate your relationship with your competitors.

To this day I'm a friend with a lot of people at Burt's Bees. I want to be friends with my competitors, because you never know what will happen. One day they may be the people most likely to buy you out, or they might want to partner with you or even want to work for you. So make friends with your competitors, and build a sincere relation-ship with them.

Lance: This is so true; our biggest and first battle is to make the naturals category huge, and this means that to some extent we are allies with our competitors. You'll never hear us bad-mouthing our competition. Burt's Bees was the leader and the instigator of taking natural to the mass market, and we owe them a huge debt for that.

Step Nine: Find a category that has room to improve.

The best way to build a better business is to find a category that is **succeeding in spite of itself.** The other brands in our category were succeeding with products that were almost twenty years old; they weren't bad, but they weren't reaching their full potential either. They weren't responding to the fast-changing environment around them. Look at the airlines; years after deregulation the "legacy carriers," United and Delta and American Airlines, had settled into a pattern of "eh." They weren't that bad, but they weren't that great either.

After United merged with Continental it had ten international hubs, and all told it operated six thousand flights a day. No wonder they were slow to react or evolve. But if you're smaller, you can come along and leapfrog your product to the head of the line. JetBlue launched with the newest planes and slickest entertainment and initially focused on a handful of major routes. They created a unique product, built up customer loyalty, and were able to avoid all the problems that drag down legacy carriers. Yes To did the same thing in the natural-beauty market.

Step Ten: Look for your niche within that category.

We learned a lot about picking products and categories in Trendtrade; one of the biggest lessons was the value of looking for fragmented players. For instance, natural beauty was completely fragmented; there was one player that had 60 percent of the market and after that the next brand had 10 percent. Budding entrepreneurs often assume that they need to create something "completely new and unique," but those are one-in-a-million ideas, and, frankly, most people are never hit by that bolt of "brilliant idea" lightning. The more useful tactic is to find a business where you can launch with a small percentage of a big market. Being a small, differentiated player in a big market can be an amazing position. In Australia we used to have two airlines: Qantas and Ansett. Virgin Blue came out of nowhere to be the third (and seemingly unnecessary) player, but then the second player, Ansett, went bust, and suddenly the upstarts had a huge niche to fill.

The natural-beauty market had Burt's Bees and no clear second-place player. Even Walgreens was looking for a "who's next?" after their success with Burt's Bees. And we came along to fill that niche. Of course, from our point of view we were very focused in going after that number two spot; we viewed Burt's Bees as our number one competitor, even when they had no clue who we were.

Another way to look at this is to seek carve-outs. Niche carve-outs create new opportunities. This is especially noticeable in the tech and online world, where the opportunity to launch start-ups and be entrepreneurial is more pronounced. An innovation company in the technology sector becomes "legacy" quicker than any other industry. Look at Google; it popped up and dominated search. After a couple of years a whole bunch of search carve-outs emerged that focused on doing one thing in the search category, but a whole lot better. Chomp, which was developed in 2010 as a search engine for mobile apps only, sold to Apple for twenty million dollars after only two years. Maybe there are similar opportunities in your industry?

Step Eleven: Know when patience is needed and when patience is bullshit.

One thing you will hear over and over as you build your ideas and your business is, "You need to be patient." We think patience is bullshit. Patience means sitting by a phone waiting for someone to return your call. Or dealing with people who say, "Let me think about it." Patience is a great spiritual practice, but if it stops you from acting, then it is stopping you from succeeding. Don't let the concept of patience stop you from getting on a plane, hustling a meeting, or finagling your way into an industry conference that you don't have a hope in hell of being invited to attend.

The flip side to this is that you've got to be somewhat patient for process. At Yes To we have to be patient while product formulations are developed, and that's about it. Our formulations are key to our integrity and success, so we give them as much time as they need. So long as we don't rush through this process, we can proceed at full velocity through all the others. Patience? Who has time for patience when there's a whole world out there to talk to about Yes To!

If we were to do this business the way the world had told us to, we would have launched in mom-and-pop stores in the naturals world, we would next have gone to Whole Foods (aka the Holy Grail), and then maybe we would have been able to get an account somewhere else. And that would all be fine, but instead of being a global business that has accounts in more than twenty-five thousand stores and is number two in our category, we'd be a struggling beauty brand sweating about covering our costs.

Don't fool yourself that you are being patient if what you are really doing is procrastinating or giving in to your unconscious fears about success.

Step Twelve: Be the most interesting person your accounts deal with.

People have used many words to describe Ido over the years, some flattering, and some rather earthier in tone. Perhaps the most perfect word to describe him is *chutzpah-dik* (or "full of chutzpah").

Chutzpah is a Yiddish term that has no direct translation to English. It denotes audacity and confidence with a good dash of humor and a lot of self-knowingness. Chutzpah can be a very attractive and valuable characteristic; it makes other people want to know who you are and be around you, if only because you're probably the most interesting person in the room.

Ido: Our first VP of sales came from a very conventional and corporate business background: Johnson & Johnson and L'Oreal. I could tell he didn't really understand what I meant when I said, "We do things differently," so I took him to a meeting at Walgreens to demonstrate. After all, I was sitting in the lobby wearing jeans, while all the other people were in gray or navy suits! As we were called to the meeting I smiled confidently and gave each person a big kiss and hug. The meeting started with a few friends talking about life as though the business discussion was secondary in nature. Needless to say we got a lot of work done, but as we left the building he turned to me and said, "That was amazing! I have been in hundreds of meetings with retailers and have never seen such a fun and productive meeting in my life." I told him, "Welcome to Yes To! I always want to hear that you had a good time at your meetings, because if you had a good time, then they had a good time, and that's only good for our business."

Step Thirteen: Start a conversation with your best customers.

Every three months Ido has a conference call with the "VICs." VIC stands for Very Important Carrots; and none of them have much in common besides the fact that they use and love Yes To products. Most of the VICs originally got in touch through Facebook, and there is no formal organization. We always knew that we wanted our customers to be so passionate about Yes To that they would willingly become our advocates and our ambassadors to the world. We have thousands of VICs who go out of their way to talk about us.

Ido: The most powerful marketing tool in the world is word of mouth. Lance and I recently went on a ski trip to Tahoe. I took my brand-new Burton board, but when I got off of the lift I discovered it was cracked at the bottom. I called Burton, told them my board was broken, and I was going for a weekend in Whistler in two days. The catch was that it was Christmas Eve. Everyone had gone for the holidays. Two hours later the rep called me back and, lo and behold, he had arranged for a board to be waiting for me on the mountainside at Whistler. And then he said that if I didn't like my new board I could take any one I wanted from the store.

Burton has a philosophy that they don't let a rider go without. That is a true way to create a loyal advocate, and I will buy another ten boards in my life—and they will all be Burton boards. I've told that story to hundreds of friends in person, and to thousands of people in auditoriums, and now I'm putting it in a book! They have an advocate for life because they treated me right. (Burton: If you need my shipping address, just let me know!) Never underestimate how powerful going out of your way for one customer can be. Whenever possible, to this day Lance and I will respond directly to customers who have a problem or a question sent in by e-mail.

Step Fourteen: Find the ten people you need to know to get your brand to the next stage.

Ido: It doesn't matter what industry you are in, or whether you are a doctor or a teacher or a businessperson. At the end of the day it will be people, not institutions or groups or companies, that determine your success. Walgreens is a massive organization, but there are only two people on the inside who are key to our success.

Over years in business we've figured out that to succeed, most endeavors need the support of ten individuals. Find those ten people and convince them that whatever you are doing is better or bigger or stronger. If you can get those ten people to buy into what you are doing, and nurture and cherish those relationships, then that's a huge part of building a massively successful career or company.

Think about it on a personal level. In your private life you probably have ten people—give or take one or two—who determine your happiness or your sadness. They could be your wife, parents, a few core friends, your kids, and your boss. If you boil your world down, you'll have a surprisingly small group of people who really matter. It's the same thing in business. I work with hundreds of people on a daily basis, but there are only ten people who I need in my professional life in order to make or break it.

Building a brand, creating a company, and fighting for success can feel huge and overwhelming. However, if you can figure out who those ten people are that you need to help you succeed, and focus on them and not worry too much about everyone else, then you've got a much greater chance of making it work. Don't tell yourself, "I need to be in Walgreens or Target," and then randomly approach anyone who seems like they might be helpful. Do a little investigative work, find out who will "get" you, who will care, and figure out a way to make that connection with them. If you sell that person on your product and get them to really care, then *they* will go out and build support for you within their organization. What will absolutely kill you is when the "right" person finds out that you've also been randomly wooing other people in their organization. Find the right person, focus on them, get them to believe, and once they do, let them sell you within their organization. Once you've got those ten people in place, nurture them. Build that relationship, and keep it happy and healthy, no matter what.

Brand Building SUMMATION

We are not the only people who've had the bright idea to go for number two in naturals. Others have tried to emulate our strategy of going into the mass market right out of the chute. They've done some things right and some things wrong. The truth is, there is a huge dose of luck and chance involved in succeeding in a business. So many things need to fall into place in order to create the secret sauce of success; all it takes is for one little element to misfire and suddenly you are in a bad position, one that might be incredibly hard to recover from.

You have a great product but your pricing is wrong? You fail. Great product but terrible distribution? You fail. No retail support? You fail. Your operations team doesn't deliver the product? You fail. You can get everything right and have a socially conscious business and yet you still fail. The key is understanding that you don't need to be perfect at everything, but you need to get the fundamentals right.

Our secret is that we got the basics right.

We created a product that people liked, that worked, and that was designed for a market we understood and were passionate about, and even though it wasn't perfect, it was *different enough for them to try.* And then we gave it everything we got!

11

The Letting Go Chapter

W E ARE GETTING TO THE end of our book, but we still have one major plot twist to share. By the beginning of 2010 we were slowly pulling out of the weeds. Now, no one really knew we had been in the weeds to begin with. Even through our darkest moments we had stayed positive and projected confidence and positivity as our default setting. We were getting tons of press and exposure, and, frankly, most people never would have guessed how close things had come to falling apart.

Without even realizing it, we were getting to that stage in a career where you sit down, evaluate what you're doing, and wonder, "Is this working for me?" On the outside, things were great. If anything, we were surprised by how big Yes To had gotten and how quickly it had gotten there. We always expected the brand to be a big deal, but we'd never expected it to become a big deal so fast. It was incredibly humbling to become the number two natural-beauty brand in the United States in five years.

The second-biggest surprise was how emotionally connected our customers were to the brand. Our customers really believed in the positivity of our message. And their belief and passion made us stop and think: Were we still living the "Yes To" message? Were we still filled with the positivity and passion that we want to encourage in our customers?

The Final Plot Twist

Ido: Success is meaningless if your personal life is falling apart. Yet living your life according to this incredibly basic and very obvious truth is somehow seen as weakness in our modern culture. Work, we are told, and the admiration and money that you earn by doing it, is everything. Your spouse is less deserving of your time and attention, your kids are less deserving of your time and attention. Forget your parents, your friends, your passions. Forget you.

We think this is bullshit.

However, there were a good few years when we found ourselves getting dragged down to a place where the bottom line was the only line. We both came close to losing people that we loved because of our insistence on putting our company first. And, truth be told, in the early days you do have to put your company first. As we both say, sometimes you need to leave and not come back till you get things done. It's acceptable to do this — in the short term. However, if you are ten years into your company and you are still essentially a stranger in your own home, or indeed your own life, then something needs to change.

Living a balanced life means being able to look at everything that matters to you — family, work, your beliefs about the world — and being able to assess when one of those things is sucking the air out of the room for the others.

We'd achieved our primary goal; we'd created a meaningful business that operates with integrity and has a strong and positive outlook for future growth and continued profitability. But I now had a brand-new daughter at home, and suddenly a big part of my love and belief and passion was for something other than Yes To. One day my daughter saw me packing for another trip and started crying. She had only just turned two, but already she knew what it meant when I pulled my Rollaboard into the hallway. Instead of feeling excited about my upcoming trip, I suddenly felt deflated. For the first time in my life I didn't want to get to the airport and get on the plane. I realized that I'd rather stay home with my daughter and my wife.

Most people have a date in their heads. This date isn't a reminder about their anniversary, or a dental appointment, or their kid's birthday. It's the date when they have enough, or have accomplished enough, in their business. In other words, retirement. But in my mind retirement was something old people do. Obviously I was too young to stop working, right? But at the same time something felt out of balance. I had everything I wanted, so why was I so miserable?

A few months after our product withdrawal had been resolved and everything was back to "normal," I was in the office in San Francisco. I was sitting at my desk, frowning at some financials that didn't make sense. I had spent the whole afternoon dealing with an HR problem that I honestly didn't know how to resolve. Tomorrow I would spend most of my day grappling with some administrative issues that couldn't be finalized without my input. I would have to hustle if I was going to be home to put my kids to bed.

On the corner of my desk I saw a folded-over piece of paper, with "Ido" written on the outside. Puzzled, I picked it up and started reading.

The letter went something like this:

> Dear Ido,
>
> I hope you do not take this letter the wrong way. But you have let me down.
>
> I know that we have not had a great deal of time together as I am in the finance team, but I felt like I needed to share this with you.

I joined Yes To because I believed in your enormous vision and true love for the brand. You have inspired me and the team to work harder and faster than any of us could have imagined. We do this because we believe that we are working on a greater mission. However, over the past few months the happy-go-lucky Ido has disappeared, and it is affecting everyone here at Yes To. We know you are going through a hard time, but we need the old Ido back.

Thanks.
Brian

For a second I was, frankly, pretty angry. How dare he? Brian was a part-time worker and yet he had the nerve to criticize the founder of the company he's working for? Who does he think he is? I'm working my ass off every day. I'm carrying the whole weight of this company on my shoulders. Everyone relies on me for their paycheck and their future. I looked up and caught a glimpse of myself in the computer monitor. For the first time, I looked haggard. My mouth was set in a semi-frown and there was a hard wrinkle running across my forehead. I realized I couldn't remember the last time I had smiled. When I forced myself to smile it felt awkward and unnatural.

As much as it kind of pissed me off to admit it, Brian was right.

I took a deep breath and pushed back from the desk. The office was quiet — I was the only one still there, breaking my long-held promise to Ronit and my daughters that I would always be home in time for dinner and the kids' baths. What the hell was going on? On some level, everything I'd wished for had come true. Lance and I had built a successful company, survived some seriously dark moments, and created a high-quality, natural product that was making the world a better place, not a worse one. Yet in my heart I felt miserable. I looked at my schedule for the next few weeks and realized that every day was filled with the minutiae of running a middle-sized, expanding business. Every decision, big or small, required my approval. As a result,

I had gone from doing what I loved and came naturally to me — sales, marketing, PR — to now spending most of my time doing work I had no natural aptitude for or interest in.

No wonder I wasn't smiling.

Brian's letter was a pivotal moment; it was, in its own way, as meaningful and important as our first meeting with Michelle at Walgreens, or the recall. It was a small nudge, but a nudge was all it took to subtly change our direction. Like all shifts in direction, it was imperceptible at first; but as time went on the change became more and more obvious.

The nudge came in the form of a moment of clarity: *I didn't want to be the CEO.* I'm OK at it but not by any means brilliant. I'm not an administrator, yet somehow my role had shifted from being an ideas and sales and marketing guy to being the guy signing off on a new photocopier or negotiating a lease renewal with the office landlord. No wonder I was depressed.

I realized that I was filling these roles because I thought being hands-on was the best thing for the company. Yet doing these jobs made me miserable, and my unhappiness was affecting my coworkers and lowering the morale of the office.

Clearly, something had to change.

The next day I held an impromptu Skype powwow with Lance. One of the great things about our partnership has always been our fundamental openness and honesty. We can say almost anything to each other and know that the other person will really listen and consider what is being said. I told him that I was not happy.

Lance: I realized that Ido was right; he needed to move out of his catchall position at Yes To and refocus himself in a way that made him happier, while not taking away from the operational flow of the company. The product withdrawal had also been a huge eye-opener; it felt like the end of the world for us. I have always prided myself on being a big-picture person, with a good perspective on life. But the truth was that we were finding it hard to move on from this unexpected hitch. I started to think about how many more of these major glitches I could handle while still taking care of everything else we were doing.

Our whole business had been built around the idea of being lean and flexible; when we launched into the United States we were literally a two-man business, and we've always stayed as small as possible. From day one we've focused on what we are good at, which is sales and marketing. Everything else we dabbled in. We dabbled in manufacturing. We dabbled in warehousing and logistics. We dabbled in R&D. As soon as we realized that we could outsource an area of our business to better-qualified people, we did so. We've always had champagne taste on a beer budget. The way we were able to sustain this was to invest the majority of our resources in the areas we were best at and outsource the rest.

This allowed us to take a risk on the functions that we knew best, such as sales and marketing, and outsource the risk on functions we knew we were more likely to mess up, such as manufacturing and warehousing and logistics.

We'd made a huge effort to build up a passionate, highly competent, and wildly enthusiastic sales team, which we think is the most important function of the business. We had appointed one or two senior people to oversee the operations, finance, and product development departments and coordinate with our outsourced suppliers. After all, what do we know about warehousing and logistics? Nothing! So why try to master someone else's game? Major retailers don't care how big or small a company is; they judge every supplier by the same performance standards whether you are a new start-up or Procter & Gamble. If you screw up, they don't care if you have two employees or two hundred; they will drop you with the speed and ferocity of a Mike Tyson uppercut.

If you're an entrepreneur, be an entrepreneur; don't try to learn a whole new set of skills once your company succeeds. Do what you are good at and hire other people to do what they are good at. Management consultants spend their time working on models that optimize functions to save a few cents per product. Entrepreneurs should spend their time working on how to perfect their trade and sell more!

At some point, there comes a time when every function of a business can be improved through outsourcing, even that of the founders. Maybe it was time to outsource the majority of Ido's and my responsibilities so we could get back to doing what we are good at and happy doing—promoting the joys of Yes To to the world!

Ido: Yes To was expanding rapidly and we knew that realistically we could expect more events like the product withdrawal. At the same time we would have to allocate more of our time to administrative tasks, HR requirements, and basic maintenance of the business. Instead of hitting the road to maintain and nurture our hard-won global retail contacts and accounts, I was stuck, staring at the computer screen. Lance was also frustrated. He was getting ready to become a brand ambassador as we launched in several new countries, but he also was chained to the desk of our San Francisco office.

Ido: We needed for one of us to focus entirely on the fast-growing international markets, Europe in particular, where we had signed an exclusive fifteen-country deal with Sephora, the world's leading premium skin-care retailer. I sat down with Lance and we had a heart-to-heart. Before we even started talking we knew exactly what we both wanted to say. It was time. Lance and I both had winged it for as long as we could in the United States and done a damn good job at it. But the stakes were getting higher. The competition was getting fiercer. The internal commitments were getting greater. We knew we now needed to look for an experienced consumer-goods CEO who could replace us and allow us to get back to what we do best: fly the Yes To flag. It was time to outsource our old jobs of CEO and COO of the company to a nonfounder.

With the support of our investors, we were able to not only out-source ourselves, but to find an absolute rock star. After months of sifting through dozens of resumes given to us by executive recruit-ment firms, we were starting to lose hope that we would find the right person to replace us. This was, of course, the most important hire we were going to make in our career to date. It's like trying to find a guardian for your child after you have decided to hand over paren-tal control of your baby. Yes To was our baby, and still was, and we now had to find and entrust it to a new guardian who would steer it through to its maturity. We spent an extensive amount of time with our private-equity investors in San Francisco dissecting exactly who would be the optimal person for this role. We called on our men-tors as well to discuss with them their thoughts and experiences from undertaking similar massive personnel changes in their companies. Talking to experienced businessmen such as our investors and men-tors gave us the confidence to make the right decision, but also with the massive changes that come along with transitioning out of these roles as we were doing.

After four long, nerve-wracking months, we met Joy Chen, a gem of a find who had spent sixteen years at Clorox as the general manager of their multibillion-dollar cleaning products division. Joy brought much-needed corporate discipline, deep consumer-goods in-sights, and organizational management skills to Yes To.

Finding a CEO to replace one founder is no easy task. Finding a CEO to replace two larger-than-life founders is Herculean! We knew appointing the wrong CEO, with all the transitional anxiety and angst it would initially create for our employees, would be disastrous if we got it wrong and had to do it a second time. Using the services of a recruitment firm, listening to your investors and mentors, and mak-ing sure they act as partial sounding boards are essential in achieving a successful outcome. It's the most significant personnel appointment you will ever make in your company — so spare no expense in finding the PERFECT candidate. In our case, when we hired Joy it changed not only our Yes To lives, but our personal lifestyles as well!

When Joy started in December 2009, it felt like a massive boulder had been taken off of our shoulders.

Lance: When Joy started, I immediately went on vacation; it had been three years since I'd taken more than a day off and it was blissful. For the first time ever I made sure that we went somewhere where there was no cell-phone coverage, Wi-Fi, or smoke signals. My family and I were fully off of the grid and it was fantastic. It was the first time I felt comfortable that our baby was in good hands. Once again Ido and I were free to start working to our strengths and passions.

I recently asked Joy what her honest impressions were of us when she first came onboard. I was expecting a detailed breakdown of the various dysfunctions in our operations, but she simply said, "You guys value relationships over business performance. All retailers value both, but business performance will always have to be there. You guys nailed the relationships side of the equation. I was able to bring in enhanced business performance; it was really the only place you were lacking."

Thank you, Joy!

The Seed Fund

Ido: Lance and I have always had a vision that Yes To would affect the world in positive ways. Part one of that vision was bringing affordable, high-quality natural-beauty products to the mass market: check! Part two was something of a bigger picture: How could we take our brand, shake it up with a little cash and a lot of passion, and create something that would benefit people outside of our natural-beauty customers?

Here's another benefit to having a brilliant wife. When we first started Yes To, Ronit suggested creating something called the Yes To

Seed Fund. The Seed Fund was originally created to help communities set up self-sustaining food sources. Our initial vision was a series of inner-city vegetable gardens and green spaces that would provide fresh produce for the local inhabitants. That sounded like a worthy and meaningful mission, and we threw ourselves into it wholeheartedly. However, as the recession hit, we were approached by a whole host of individuals and small charities that were struggling and desperately needed cash.

Since we are both pretty softhearted, our initial mission of supporting small gardens quickly diversified into supporting a random group of small nonprofits. Ronit took to calling the Seed Fund the Whatever Made Ido and Lance Cry Fund.

Finally, we realized that if we wanted to be effective, we needed one specific mission; after all, we were working with a fixed budget. Spending five hundred dollars here or a thousand dollars there ultimately wasn't that effective. Instead, we decided to invest all of our budget on one project and see if we could make a meaningful difference that way. We reached out to the Very Important Carrots, asked what we should do, and the number one project they suggested was something that would improve nutrition for children.

We teamed up with a group called the Environmental Media Association, or EMA, that mobilizes the entertainment industry in educating people about environmental issues, which, in turn, inspires them to take action. We started planting organic fruit and veggie gardens in schools in Los Angeles. We were able to get some celebrity support (always useful when you are trying to raise money and interest!) when people like Nicole Richie, Rosario Dawson, and Daryl Hannah pitched in to help.

The first few gardens were a hit, and we decided to expand the program nationally. Because that's a big commitment, we partnered with retailers like Whole Foods, who helped us get the word out about the program and encouraged schools to apply for a grant. We now have seed fund programs all over the States. We've also partnered with two amazing women via an organization called Mama Hope to take the program overseas and start helping kids in Africa. Our micro-farms in Africa are phenomenal: We found an efficient, effective way to plant organic produce around the schools there, and our first projects feed ten thousand kids a day. We hope to reach tens of thousands of kids on a daily basis.

Why does any of this matter?

Look around you; these are challenging times. If we are going to pull through on a local, regional, or international level, then we all have to pitch in, *now*. Giving back has to be part of your company's mission statement, no matter what your personal beliefs, your politics, or your passions. I strongly believe that we in the business world have an obligation — and an opportunity — to help others. Lance and I have two wonderful children each. Our kids get the best food, education, and health care money can buy. I would literally do anything for my children, and I know that the homeless mother, the out-of-work father, and the inner-city teacher all feel the same way about their kids. If I can help them take care of their kids, that's a wonderful thing.

What's Your Mission?

You don't have to start big. Nor do you even need to start by giving money; our first foray into giving back was volunteering, as a group, at a local afterschool program in Tel Aviv. We did it more as a bonding exercise than anything else, but the sheer joy of interacting with the kids pushed us to want to do more. Do a monthly half day of volunteering, find local schoolkids you can mentor, offer assistance to their parents. Pitch in. Whatever your area of expertise, find a way to give back a little to your local community. You might not think it, but devoting your time and your employees' time to volunteering can be exactly the same as giving a monetary amount to charity. You are effectively paying for your employees to be there and not working in the office. There is a monetary and an opportunity cost associated with that, and most companies that like to quantify and market how much they give each year include these amounts in their charitable contributions. Remember, though: This doesn't mean sending employees out after hours or on weekends to "volunteer"!

The most important thing is that regardless of where you end up focusing your attention, you need to do it in an authentic and real way, and it has to be something that your coworkers are fired up about. It is great for the founder or CEO to have a mission, but if the rest of the team doesn't support it, it is pointless. One of our employees used to work for a man who was obsessed with attaining "platinum donor" status with a well-known national charity. His motivation was the potentially lucrative connections of the local board members, and he made it known that any employee who didn't donate generously was in danger of losing their job. Not the best way to garner your employees' support for your cause!

Giving Back, the Yes To Way

One of the things that I love about our company is how fast we can move when we really need to. The decision-making hierarchy at Yes To is very quick; the turnaround time can be mere hours if we feel like something is right for the brand. This allows us to respond really quickly when we see a chance to help and we know in our hearts that it is the right thing to do. Because we're small, there is also a high level of internal accountability; we all want to take ownership of an idea and execute it well. Eventually, we want to have a dedicated department within Yes To that is solely responsible for the Seed Fund.

All this means that as soon as we decided to really go for it with the Seed Fund, we really went for it. About a week after our VIC conference call we had a budget, a plan, and a basic structure for how our employees would be involved.

Here are our ideas for the kinds of things to think about as you move forward:

Right at your company's birth, begin to think about how and where you will give back. Weave the idea of giving back to your community into your corporate DNA. Make it integral to your overall mission. Look at companies that have launched with a "one-for-one" strategy, for instance, companies like TOMS Shoes and Warby Parker that donate a pair of shoes or glasses, respectively, to the needy for every pair sold.

Make sure there is a clear link between your charitable work and what your brand stands for. If your company makes clothes or other items out of cotton, look at ways to support fair-trade cotton or clean-water programs. Find a connection between your corporate and charitable worlds, even if it means acknowledging a potential negative in your own business model.

Shout about your program loud and proud from the rooftop! Enthusiasm and passion are infectious. Let your family, competitors, friends, and the press know what you are doing and how they can get involved. These charitable programs are like a game of follow the leader. Once one person does it, everyone else will too. The end goal is to make charitable giving from corporations not an exception but a given.

Authenticity is key; the general public can smell when a brand is not being genuine, and then your "greenwashing" will do you more harm than good. Nothing makes me more irate than those phony "green" ads put out by oil and coal companies. People are smart; don't try to trick them.

You *can* make a difference, even if you are a small one- or two-person entity. Time and effort are often more valuable than money.

Make sure you have a culture that makes people want to spend time together. This is part of a bigger picture of shaping the social culture of your organization, but it has huge ramifications for building an effective charitable program. After all, being forced to "volunteer" with a random group of coworkers is not appealing, but volunteering with friends is a lot of fun, and if you can give your employees that opportunity, they will jump at it.

Stay focused. When we first started we were 100 percent unfocused; there was no rhyme or reason to our charitable endeavors. Our lack of a message lessened our impact as a force for good. Talk to your customers to identify a charitable initiative that really aligns with who you are and what you represent. Then commit to it.

Business is full of big secrets that you don't learn at business school. One of the biggest is that it's one thing to become successful; learning to enjoy that success is the next big challenge. Think about it. At what point in your career will you have "enough" success? When will your priorities shift from attaining more to being happy with what you have? Or look at it another way: What does success look like to you? I have friends who won't be happy until they have hundreds of millions in the bank. I have other friends who have found their perfect spot in the world by living in intentional meditative communities. If they met, each would think the other was crazy, but they are both working toward a fulfilling and meaningful life on their own terms.

Ido: When my mom joined Herbalife, her definition of success would have been something along the lines of "earning enough money to stop my family from falling apart." Eventually that evolved into larger financial goals, but she knew she'd succeeded when she was able to look at us and see that we had gotten back our positivity and belief in our future. Her definition of success was saving her family, and she succeeded and then some.

When Lance and I were working in Trendtrade, our goal was to make millions. Those financial outcomes have remained important as our lives have evolved, but what is even more important is the ability to lead a good life, enjoy your days, and have the people you love by your side.

Your definition of success might be more modest. Suppose you want to make a few thousand dollars in passive income a month; that's great. Perhaps it's a creative goal — you want to learn the skills to build a house. Or a personal or spiritual goal. Whatever it is, be clear about what you are really looking for. It's possible that success will look a little different in real life than it did in your imagination.

When our first daughter was born, I told myself that my kids would understand if work was my priority because I was doing it all for them, but the truth is, my kids *don't* understand. They don't care about Yes To (yet); they don't notice that we live in a nice house or have great health-care insurance; all they really know is that it makes them incredibly sad when I go on a trip. They want their dad. Realizing how my kids felt was huge; if I was willing to say "so what," I could probably be Donald Trump in forty years, but I'm not willing to trade a happy family for that kind of success. All the supermodel trophy wives in the world aren't worth that. My vision of success had to change a little as my life changed. And so will yours.

Lance: The only feeling that won't change is that of regret. Regret can ruin your life; it will play with your mind and destroy your confidence and trust in people, especially if you use it as the justification for why you are not fulfilled or happy with your life as it is. The number of times we have sat listening to the woes and career frustrations of friends and colleagues who all wish they could "leave their secure jobs but they have a family and a mortgage" is astounding. Yes, it is a huge risk to leave a secure job. Yes, it is a huge risk to start from scratch or join a new start-up. Figure out what kind of risk you can live with and take those chances. And know that when you are lying on your deathbed, you can look up and say, "I did everything I wanted to do in life, for myself and for the people I loved the most." If you can't see yourself saying that, then figure out what's stopping you. Stop talking about "doing it" and start working toward your most honest, authentic, and passionate goals.

Ido: The shift that took us from being executives to founders, and the creation of the Seed Fund, are two big parts of a three-part story. The third part is something harder to put our fingers on; it's a good vibe, or a happy, united feeling. It's one of those things that is sometimes easier to express in another language; the word I want may be bonhomie. Maybe it's simply emphasizing a positive corporate culture above a relentless pursuit of profits. I don't think either Lance or I realized how special and rare the atmosphere is at Yes To, at least not until we came close to losing it in the fallout from the product withdrawal. I was willing to change how I do things to keep my family happy, and I'll do the same for my work family too.

We truly love our company and our employees. That's kind of a rare thing; how many companies have you worked for where you felt that kind of mutual affection and happiness? Of course, we still have our problems, but even the greatest sprinters hit the hurdles occasionally. If you are honest about your screw-ups and add in the "good" component, people will love you every step of the way.

Entrepreneurship can be a very lonely road; you may lose some friends along the way. When we first started the company, I called up my closest friends and told them I was disappearing for a while — I love you, but you won't see me till I achieve certain goals. When I finally resurfaced, some of my old friends were no longer there; they were hurt and angry and felt abandoned. I understood their feelings, but the friends who *were* still there are the closest and most loved friends I have. Even more importantly, the same applies to your life partner. We both met our wives before we started Yes To, and they've experienced all the highs and lows of starting a company. It has never shaken their confidence or support for us; on the contrary, they have contributed even more in putting their own career aspirations on hold so we could chase after ours. Our wives were copywriters, product creators, idea generators, and lab-sample guinea pigs. There were plenty of shaky times when we could have lost our entire business and all the effort, savings, and dreams along with it. But Ronit and Loren have stuck with us for the entire journey and acted as pillars of support and strength throughout.

If you want to build it big, fast, and good, surround yourself with other people who are fighting and striving to accomplish the same thing; their motivation and energy will drive and push you. There are thousands of businesses out there happy to build things slow, steady, and small. And more power to them! But if you have a different vision, then find people whose ambition aligns with your own and gives you a sense of kinship as you build.

A Bee's Perspective

One of the fun parts about writing this book has been approaching friends, investors, coworkers, and competitors and asking, "So, what do you really think about us?"

A few weeks before the book was due, we figured what the heck — and shot off an e-mail to John Replogle, the former CEO of Burt's Bees. I'm proud to call John my former biggest competitor, a great friend, and an inspiration in both business and life, so it was exciting and humbling when he responded with his thoughts about what makes Yes To work, and why. Now, this isn't just a massive pat on my own back. John's answers (like Scott's and Michelle's) are packed with the kind of wisdom that comes only from looking from the outside in. Have a read and see what you can learn from our biggest competitor. Maybe there's something here that applies to your own business and life.

Yes To first hit my radar when I was CEO of Burt's Bees. I walked down an aisle of Walgreens to admire our brand and *wham*, there was this bright orange new brand selling a natural body butter on a BOGO (buy one, get one free) deal. Of course, I couldn't resist. I bought one and got one free, bringing one home and one back to our R&D lab to study. When I got home to my wife and four daughters, I simply put the product on the counter and awaited their reply. They admired the fun and approachable packaging. They opened the lid to a great fragrance and dug their fingers right in to scoop up some "carrot butter."

They loved it. I wondered where this was made and who was behind it. I learned that it was made in Israel with "Dead Sea minerals." That was unique positioning and clearly an unusual sourcing strategy. How on earth could these guys make a quality product, ship it from Israel, sell it at Walgreens at a reasonable price, and then sell it on a BOGO and still make money? It was perplexing and appeared to defy the rules. Clearly, there was a unique team behind this new company. Who was it? What were they up to? Didn't they understand the rules of beauty? What on earth was going on?

After doing a bit of desk research, I decided I had to know more. I called the beauty buyer at Walgreens and set up an appointment. Not wanting to show my hand, I set up a "routine" business check-in as Walgreens was quickly becoming one of our very top customers. I flew out to Chicago with a binder full of questions, just looking to learn more.

When I asked the buyer about Yes To, what I learned began to both worry and thrill me. Yes To was on fire. Their body butter was one of the best-selling stock-keeping units, not only in natural but in all of body care. They had done an incredible job building buzz and buy-in with Walgreens management and had agreed to an exclusive deal. These guys had come to play hardball. I visited a few Walgreens stores in the Chicago area to see if I could learn more. I wanted to see how strong their shelf execution was and whether they had made inroads with the

Walgreens beauty advisors that worked in each store. It took me about ten seconds to find an answer. I walked up the beauty aisle and there was a bright orange display of Yes To and a shelf full of products including their BOGO body butter. I sought out the beauty advisor, who warmly greeted me with a bright orange beam in her smile. Yes, they had gotten to her as well! Who the heck were these guys and how did they pull this off? My curiosity was piqued.

A few weeks later, after speaking to everyone who would take my call, I finally learned that a really unique guy was behind this juggernaut of a brand. His name was Ido (never heard of that one before) and he was an Israeli who'd grown up in Australia and was now traveling around the world building this brand, though he considered San Francisco his U.S. home. Having learned his identity, I had to orchestrate a meeting. And it didn't take long. I was a speaker at an upcoming industry meeting and I learned that Ido would be there. A mutual friend made arrangements for us to meet and I looked forward to learning more about this mystery man.

Our first meeting was memorable. Along comes this bright orange ball of energy with a shaven head, a lean frame, a broad smile, and an unusual accent that flowed from his lips at an astounding rapid-fire clip.

"Hey ya, you're da Burt's guy, I'm Ido," he said. Huh? Oh, he's speaking English! I'd never met a guy quite like this. After a few minutes of conversation, it was clear that we'd become fast friends. Ido, it turns out, was a passionate entrepreneur with a vision to change the world for the better. We connected on core values and a belief in the power of business to make a positive change. His humor was disarming. His passion was infectious and his ability to schmooze—I believe that's Yiddish for building affectionate rapport—was priceless.

After a few hours of talking, we agreed to meet that night at the conference cocktail reception and party. As we worked the crowd, I was struck by the thought that Ido was the greatest self-promoter I had ever met. He had courage and brass balls and would speak to anyone at any time about any subject. He was also a lot of fun and could hold quite a few drinks for such a slender frame. That night we talked business and enjoyed life. We hit the casino-night event, bet large, won big, and walked away with prizes as well as a burgeoning friendship. This Ido character, I knew, would become an important person in my life: a competitor, a comrade, a friend, and an inspiration.

Looking back, it's hard to believe that Yes To made it. Most companies fail due to a lack of vision and ambition. This wasn't the case with Yes To—in fact, it was just the opposite. Ido was driving, forming, and creating Yes To at such a breakneck speed I was certain it would fall apart due to the pace. But it didn't! He rolled out new products in three months' time when it took the industry two years. He moved manufacturing from Israel to the United States and, in the process, overhauled most of the formulas, creating a cleaner, more natural formula. He forged new customer partnerships around the world. He built a PR machine and developed first-name relationships with all the key beauty editors. Ido was everywhere and he was doing all of this with a lean, mean team. It was simply breathtaking. Ido would promise the world and he and his team would always find a way to make it work. Within ten months he had accomplished what it takes most companies ten years to achieve. Yes To was a force shaping the industry and Ido was a man on a mission.

Yes To quickly became the complement to Burt's Bees in the natural category. While Burt's was the clear leader, whether "natural" was truly a category had long been a question. There were nearly eight hundred small natural brands, each vying to make it in the mainstream market. Few of them managed to get traction and none of them had been able to carve out a credible master-brand platform that appealed to the broader consumer market. Then along came Yes To. With a "fast follow" innovation strategy, they quickly studied what other brands were doing effectively, with a keen eye on Burt's, and copied those brands, bringing the same product platforms to market but with their own unique twist.

Yes To brought growth and energy to the category and helped to anchor most natural personal-care sets as a viable master brand. Despite pissing us off many times as they copied our product innovation, we realized that Yes To's growth was an overall net positive as they drew more customers and consumers into the natural movement. Together, Burt's growth accelerated as Yes To blossomed. This strange relationship quickly proved to be a positive, powerful partnership.

Conclusion: Riding the Momentum

W E GIVE TONS OF TALKS to aspiring innovators, leaders of Fortune 500 companies, and entrepreneurs. While we're talking, we look at the faces of the hundreds, sometimes thousands of hopeful, inspired, and passionate dreamers in the audience. We have thirty minutes, maybe, to lay out a road map to making it.

We both grew up within spitting distance of the greatest beaches in the world, and we love surfing. Nothing quite beats the feeling of catching that wave. When you're sitting on the sand, it looks effortless and graceful, but the reality is that for every kid making it look easy, there are twenty kids getting creamed in the surf. Creating your own business is a bit like swimming for those waves — you've got seconds! Unless you start swimming at the right moment, you'll screw up. Either you'll be left in the wave's wake or you'll be pummeled under its crest. Surfing is timing, instinct, experience, and blind faith all mashed up together in a split-second reaction.

If we have to sum up our "secret," it would be our ability to feel the almost imperceptible shifts in the water we're paddling around in. There is a counterintuitive skill to catching a wave; you have to commit to going forward just as you feel the water start to pull you back.

Knowing how to do this is somewhat instinctual, and you have to trust your gut when it tells you to paddle. We caught our wave when we committed to Yes To.

If you stop swimming, striving, and moving forward for even a millisecond, in business as in surfing, you will miss that wave and get sucked back. All you can do is paddle as hard as possible, beat that wave, and get ahead of it. And here's the tricky part: Just as you think you've caught the wave, your brain instinctively slows down a little, and suddenly you're slipping backwards down the flank of the wave. You almost had it, but you lost it. You've got to push through that instinct that tells you to slow down. You've got to push through your body's protective instincts and keep going.

When we started Yes To, we felt in our heart of hearts that we'd caught our wave, and we weren't going to let anyone or anything stop us from riding it. No matter what. We are still out there paddling every single day. Of course, at our advanced age and with Yes To rolling under its own steam, we are no longer the guys going for the big waves. Maybe we are the guys on the stand-up paddleboards instead.

Ido: Or, in Lance's case, the guy dog-paddling after his board, pretending he can't hear his kids laughing at him.

Lance: [Censored.]

Hopefully, this book has inspired you to *Get Big Fast and Do More Good*. There are plenty of people who've built it big and slow, and they deserve a lot of recognition as well. Fast can mean different things to different people, but if you want to build something fast, you have to be prepared to get in the water and swim. And when you see a promising wave, make like hell for it. Never say, "I'll wait for the next one."

Acknowledgments

From very early on in our partnership it became a tradition that after any key event or memorable experience in our business career, one of us would loudly exclaim, "Now that's definitely going into the book!" Eight years on from our first meeting at the MLC Centre in Sydney, where we decided to go into partnership together, we sat down in a pub on a brisk, sunny, wintery afternoon during a visit to Melbourne, Australia, and decided to finally put our thoughts to paper. It was the time to reflect upon not only what we had learned and experienced but also the people who had helped us get there and shared with us each and every one of those experiences along the way.

First, we would like to thank Caroline Greeven, who expertly weaved together hundreds of hours of our interviews, ramblings, laughter, arguments, and adventures to create a coherent and perfect reflection of our story. Caroline quickly deciphered our mixed accents and vastly different tones to accurately find our joint voice and bring our book to life. We could not have asked for a better person to work with to make this book a reality. Similarly, without the business savvy and encouragement of James Reilly, our literary agent, this book would not be a reality. Thank you James and David Moldawer for believing enough in our story so we could tell it to the world.

Our story and experience could not have been possible without the contributions of our amazing team, retail partners, and investors. There are far too many people to thank here who have contributed immensely to the progress and success of Yes To. From the initial blood and toil invested by our first employees in Israel and Chicago to the sensational team we have now in San Francisco, we cannot thank you all enough for your hard work and dedication—you are all truly family!

Absolutely none of this would have been possible if it weren't for two people who have believed in us from the very first time we brought them the Yes To opportunity. Thank you guys for "backing our horse" and your unshakeable support.

As we have said throughout the book, we cannot emphasize enough the importance and value of balancing work life with your family life and friendships. None of our sacrifices would have been tenable without the support and love of our families and friends. Our parents, Dan and Yaffa, Peter and Shirley, supported us emotionally, consistently, and, at times, even financially, always believing in our dreams and challenging us to shoot for the stars no matter how crazy the path ahead seemed. Our brothers, Itai and Larry, and sisters, Tessa and Stacey, have been our biggest supporters since we were cheeky kids with huge dreams and little else. Likewise Ev, Wendy, Gid, Disco, Lou-Lou, Mark, Addi, Tiff, Josh, Katie, Jo, Shai, Adrian, Ilan, Daphna, Jony, Yonette, Keeno, Brucie, Lachie, Stef, Al, and Lols—our lifelong friends who have put up with our ups and downs and always been there as mates when we needed them most.

Most significant of all are our wives and kids—Ronit and Loren and the pride of our lives, Zoe, Emi, Ethan, and Claudia. We both met our wives before we started Yes To, and they've experienced all the highs and lows of starting a company. It has never shaken their confidence or support for us; on the contrary, they have contributed even more in putting their own career aspirations on hold so we could chase after ours. Our wives were copywriters, product creators, idea generators, and lab-sample guinea pigs. There were plenty of shaky times when we could have lost our entire business and all the effort, savings, and dreams along with it. But Ronit and Loren have stuck with us for the entire journey and acted as pillars of support and strength throughout. Our kids are the reason we kept on fighting through the tough times. Not only because we didn't want to disappoint them but also because they gave us perspective that no business experience—positive or negative—can trump: that of having the love and time to spend with your kids in this world.

We have loved every moment of developing this book and feel blessed to have been in the position to write it. We sincerely hope you enjoy it as well and get the value you deserve to live out your dreams and aspirations. We promise that we will continue to shoot for the stars and never stop thinking big, fast, and good!

Let's continue the conversation at www.GetBigFastandDoMoreGood.com and on Twitter @idoleffler and @lancekalish.

Index